EASY-TO-BUILD
OUTDOOR
& DECK PROJECTS

From the Editors of *Weekend Woodcrafts* magazine
Rob Joseph and Linda Hendry

An EGW Publishing book—Distributed by Fox Chapel Publishing

Fox
Chapel Publishing

Alan Giagnocavo
Publisher

Gretchen Bacon
Assistant Book Editor

Ayleen Stellhorn
Project Editor

Troy Thorne
Cover Design

Jon Deck & Suzy Creighton
Layout Design

Easy-to-Build Outdoor & Deck Projects is a compilation of projects featured in *Weekend Woodcrafts* magazine. The patterns contained herein are copyrighted by the authors. Readers who purchase this book may make up to three photocopies of each pattern for personal use. The patterns themselves, however, are not to be duplicated for resale or distribution under any circumstances. Any such copying is a violation of copyright law.

ISBN 1–56523–249–6

To learn more about the other great books
from Fox Chapel Publishing, or to find a
retailer near you, call toll-free 1-800-457-9112
or visit us at **www.FoxChapelPublishing.com.**

Printed in China
10 9 8 7 6 5 4 3 2 1

Library of Congress Cataloging-in-Publication Data

Joseph, Robert.
    Easy-to-build outdoor & deck projects / Rob Joseph and Linda
Hendry. — East Petersburg, PA : Fox Chapel Publishing, © 2005.

        p. cm.

        "From the editors of Weekend Woodcrafts magazine."
        "An EGW Publishing book—distributed by Fox Chapel Publishing."
        ISBN: 1-56523-249-6

        1. Outdoor furniture. 2. Woodwork. 3. Furniture making.
    4. Decorative arts. I. Hendry, Linda. II. Title. III. Easy-to-build
    outdoor and deck projects. IV. Weekend woodcrafts.

TT197.5.O9 J67 2005
749/.8—dc22   0501

Because working with wood and other materials inherently includes the risk of injury and damage, this book cannot guarantee that creating the projects in this book is safe for everyone. For this reason, this book is sold without warranties or guarantees of any kind, expressed or implied, and the publisher and the author disclaim any liability for any injuries, losses, or damages caused in any way by the content of this book or the reader's use of the tools needed to complete the projects presented here. The publisher and the author urge all woodworkers to thoroughly review each project and to understand the use of all tools before beginning any project.

Contents

Tools

Table Saw – (Stationary) The 10" table saw is probably the most common and widely used tool in a wood shop. The table saw is mainly used to make straight cuts with the grain, called ripping. It can also be used in a number of ways to make dadoes, rabbets, grooves, and bevels. Crosscuts can be made with the use of a miter gauge.

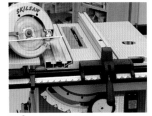

Circular Saw – (Portable) A circular saw makes straight cuts with the use of a straight edge and saw horses. Nice to have, but they can be heavy.

Drill/Driver – (Portable) A drill/driver is a tool that everyone needs. There are many battery operated models available, along with the corded. These are used to drill holes and to drive screws. Works in the place of the hand-held screwdriver.

Drill Press – (Stationary) The drill press, whether a tall stationary one or the table-top version, is a great tool, although not a necessity. It's easier to drill a straight, more accurate hole when using a drill press. Used for drilling, countersinking, mortising (with an attachment), and sanding, with the addition of a drum sanding bit.

Router – (Stationary) The router is a very a useful tool. A router comes separate from the table, but when installed in a router table it is considered a stationary tool. Routers can put those decorative edges on your piece, round over edges, make rabbets, dadoes, grooves, and chamfers. Now, you can even make biscuit slots with the use of the right bit. If you can get a convertible router, one that can go from a standard router to a plunge router, you'll be able to do almost anything.

Plunge Router – (Portable) We show using a portable plunge router for making hanging slots. This can be done with a router table, just plan ahead and make the slot before any curves are cut on the piece. It's much easier to have a straight edge to hold against the fence.

Band Saw – (Stationary) The band saw is used mainly to cut curves. The smaller the width of the blade, the tighter the curve. Band saws can cut thicker wood than a scroll saw or a jigsaw. And with a wide blade installed you can use a band saw to re-saw thicker lumber to get thinner pieces, saving on the cost of lumber.

Scroll Saw – (Stationary) A scroll saw is good for making inside cuts in projects (the band saw cannot do this). It works well on smaller pieces, but is limiting in the thickness of wood used, usually nothing over 1" thick.

Saber Saw – (Portable) The saber saw, also known as a jig saw, is an alternative to use when cutting curves, if the curves are not too small. It's good to use a saber saw on larger projects where using a stationary tool would not be safe.

Finishing Sander – (Portable) Although called a finishing sander, this type of sander can take you through all grits of sandpaper. My favorite is an orbital sander; it fits the hand well, and there's more control.

Biscuit Joiner – (Portable) The biscuit joiner is a great tool for joining wood together. The biscuit joiner cuts a slot. With the addition of a store-bought biscuit and glue, you have a good strong joint along the butted edges of two pieces.

Brad Nailer – (Portable) A brad nailer is fun and fast. Brad nailers come in various sizes, and are either electric or pneumatic (used with an air compressor). Size will depend on your type of projects. But one that can accommodate several sizes of brads is best.

Miter Saw – (Portable) A miter saw is used mainly for cutting angles. They are also used to cut across the grain for wood length. There are several types; a basic miter saw that makes straight cuts and angles, or a compound miter saw where the blade not only pivots, but also tilts.

Miter Box with Saw – (Hand Tool) A miter box is a small table-top tool used with a hand saw that usually comes as a set. As simple as a wooden box with angles cut in it, or a larger one made of metal. A miter box and saw can cut angles, just not as accurately or as fast as a larger miter saw.

Planer – (Stationary) A planer is used to shave down the thickness of the wood. For example, a ¾" stock can be planed to achieve a ½"- ¼" thickness, which gives you much more flexibility when building projects. Re-sawing on a band saw and sanding smooth is an option in some cases.

Supplies

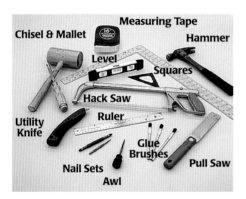

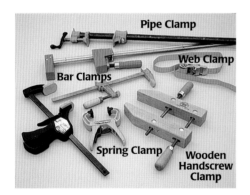

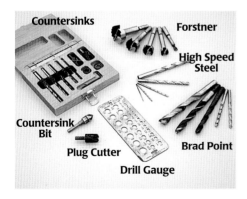

While the power tools are necessary, there are other tools and supplies that are frequently used on all projects. It's a good idea to keep these on hand too:

1. **First-Aid kit** – basics, along with eye wash and tweezers.

2. **Fire Extinguisher** – for type ABC fires. (A) wood, trash, and paper, (B) volatile finishing materials, liquid, and grease, (C) electrical equipment

3. **Double-Sided Tape** – to adhere patterns or gang wood together before cutting or drilling.

4. **Wood Glue** – sets up faster than white glue. Comes in dark color for darker woods.

5. **Instant Glue** – for wood-on-wood or wood-on-metal adhesion.

6. **Spray Adhesive** – keeps patterns on wood when scroll sawing.

7. **Wood Putty** – fills nail holes before finishing.

8. **Awl** – great for marking hole locations. The mark left from the awl will keep the drill from wandering.

9. **Steel Ruler** – a reliable ruler is a must.

10. **Nail Set** – a tool used to set the nail under the surface of the wood.

11. **Hammer** – a must in any shop.

12. **Chisel and Mallet** – to square or clean up corners after routing.

13. **Square** – keeping things square is important.

14. **Measuring Tape** – easy to keep handy for those longer pieces.

15. **Hack Saw** – needed to cut metal rods.

16. **Glue Brushes** – to spread glue on larger surfaces.

17. **Utility Knife** – good all purpose tool.

18. **Pull Saw** – to trim dowels flush.

19. **Clamps** – you can never have enough clamps. Get a variety of sizes and styles (bar, pipe, spring, web).

20. **Wooden Handscrew Clamp** – great for holding small pieces when drilling without marring the wood.

21. **Drill Bit Set** – a good set of drill bits in a variety of sizes. Brad point and Forstners are good. A drill gauge helps determine diameters.

22. **Countersink Bit** – used to countersink a hole so the screw head will set under the surface of the wood. A plug cutter to cut plugs for the countersunk holes.

23. **Scissors** – for cutting patterns, tape, etc.

24. **Sandpaper** – 80, 100, 150, 220 grits for a good variety.

EASY-TO-BUILD
OUTDOOR
& DECK PROJECTS

Redwood Picnic Table with Benches

Dimensions

Step 1 - Cut the top (A), top supports (B), leg cross supports (D), and underneath center supports (E) to the dimensions given in the material list. Use the table saw and radial arm saw to cut each piece.

25-Degree Miters

Step 2 - Cut the legs (C) to the dimensions given in the material list. Use the miter saw to miter a 25-degree angle on the ends of all four legs. Refer to side view drawing for proper orientation.

45-Degree Miters

Step 3 - The top blanks fasten into the two end top supports. Measure down 1" from the top edge and knock off each corner with a 45-degree miter cut.

End Supports

Step 4 - The legs are fastened to the end top supports with the bolts (O). Refer to the side view drawing for bolt locations. Legs are centered under the table with a 2" space between them. Mark and pre-drill through both the top supports and legs using a ⅜" bit.

Fastening

Step 5 - Fasten the legs to the top end supports with the bolts, washers, and nuts. Use a couple of wrenches to tighten each bolt.

Pre-Drilling/Fastening

Step 6 - Miter the leg cross supports' ends to 25 degrees. Place the cross supports against the legs and clamp when the ends are flush with the outside edge of the legs. Refer to the side view drawing for the three bolt hole locations. Pre-drill through the cross supports and into the legs with a ⅜" bit. Bolt the pieces together, as shown in the photo inset.

Material List	Wood	Quantity	T x W x L
Table			
A top	redwood	6	1½" x 5½" x 72"
B top supports	redwood	3	1½" x 3½" x 33"
C legs	redwood	4	1½" x 5½" x 33"
D leg cross supports	redwood	2	1½" x 5½" x 30"
E underneath center supports	redwood	2	1½" x 5½" x 27⅝"
F center support blocks	redwood	4	1½" x 1½" x 11"
Benches			
G seats	redwood	4	1½" x 5½" x 72"
H legs	redwood	8	1½" x 3½" x 19"
I leg cross supports	redwood	4	1½" x 3½" x 16"
J seat supports	redwood	4	1½" x 3½" x 11"
K underneath center supports	redwood	4	1½" x 3½" x 19"
L center support blocks	redwood	8	1½" x 1½" x 6"
Supply List			
M nuts for table		20	½"
N washers for table		40	1¼" diam. x ½"
O bolts for table		20	⅜" x 4"
P lag screws for table		4	⅜" x 4"
Q lag screws for benches		4	⅜" x 3½"
R wood screws exterior		92	#8 x 2½"
S nuts for benches		24	⅜"
T washers for table and benches		60	1" diam. x ⅜"
U bolts for benches		24	⅜" x 4"
V double-sided tape			
W Olympic Clear Wood Preservative			

Our picnic table and benches were made out of redwood, and being from the west coast it seemed appropriate; however, cedar or teak can be used if redwood is hard to come by.

Top Middle Support

Step 7 - The top support for the middle lies flat against the bottom side of the top in final assembly. Measure down from the top of one end ½" and miter each end at 45-degrees.

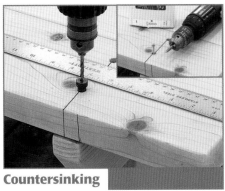

Countersinking

Step 8 - Flip the top blanks face side down. Clamp the top blanks together tightly. Locate the center and screw the middle top support across each top blank with miters facing up. Apply two screws (R) for each blank. Refer to the front view drawing for proper placement.

Step 9 - Place the clamped tabletop onto the leg assemblies. Refer to the front view drawing for proper overhang. Draw a line across the top blanks centered over the top end supports. Using a #6 countersinking bit, countersink two holes to a depth of ⅜" into each top blank. Use the wood screws (R) to fasten table in place, as shown in the inset.

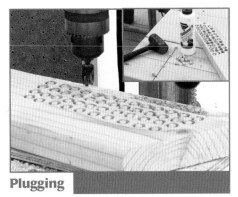

Plugging

Step 10 - Use the drill press with a ⅜" plug cutter to make the wooden plugs that cover the screw heads.

Side View Table

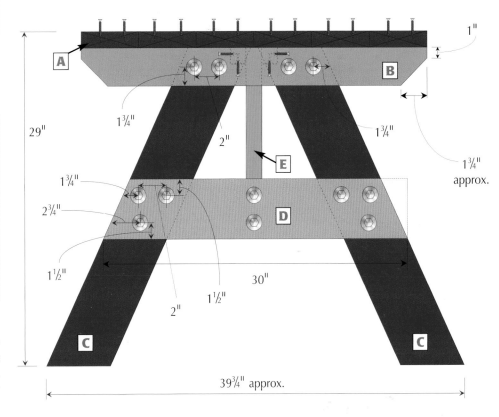

Center Supports

Step 11 - Cut 45-degree miters on the ends of both underneath center supports. Dry-fit each support and mark a line across using a straight edge to determine how much material is to be removed. Remove the material with a hand saw.

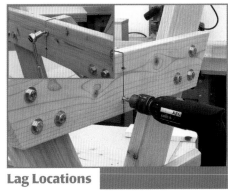

Lag Locations

Step 12 - Locate the center on the leg cross support and pre-drill two evenly spaced holes for the lag screws (P). Fasten the center supports to the cross supports with the lag screws and washers (T).

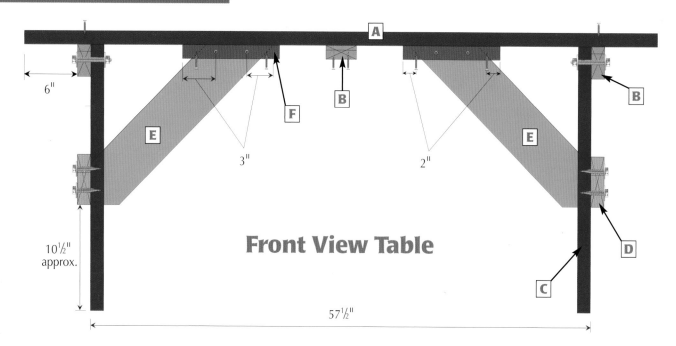

Front View Table

6"

10½"
approx.

3"

2"

57½"

A

B

F

E

B

D

C

E

Support Blocks

Step 13 - Cut the center support blocks (F) to the dimensions given in the material list. Place the blocks against the center supports and space four holes evenly, two across the sides and two on the top. Use the drill press to pre-drill each hole, as shown in the photo inset.

Fastening

Step 14 - Stagger each block slightly and use the screws (R) to fasten each block.

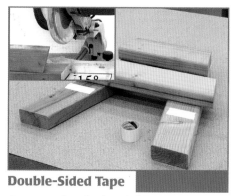

Double-Sided Tape

Step 15 - Cut the bench legs (H), leg cross supports (I), and seat supports (J) to the dimensions in the material list. Cut the ends of each piece with the miter saw set to 15 degrees, as shown in the photo inset. Use double-sided tape and place the seat supports across the legs flush with the legs' top edges. Place the leg cross supports across the legs at the point where the ends of the supports are flush with the outside edge of the legs.

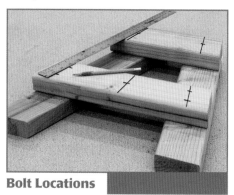

Bolt Locations

Step 16 - Refer to the bench side view drawing for bolt hole and lag screw locations. Transfer the locations to each leg assembly.

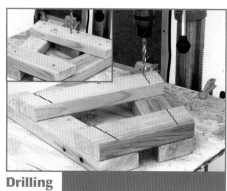

Drilling

Step 17 - Use the drill press with a ⅜" bit to drill each through hole.

Rounding Over

Step 18 - Label each leg assembly accordingly and disassemble. Use the router and a ½" round-over bit to ease the edges of the leg pieces. Sand each piece through 150-grit.

Front View Bench

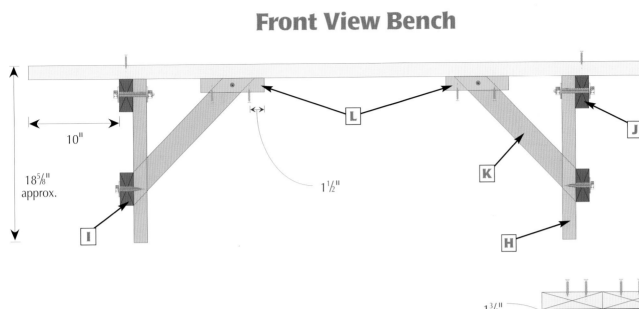

- G
- J
- L
- K
- I
- H
- 10"
- 18⅝" approx.
- 1½"

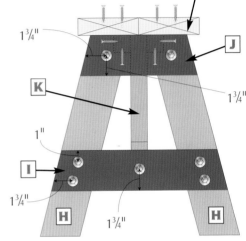

- G
- J
- K
- I
- H
- 1¾"
- 1¾"
- 1"
- 1¾"
- 1¾"

Side View Bench

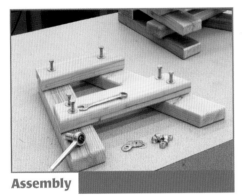

Assembly

Step 19 - Use the nuts (S), washers (T), and bolts (U) to fasten each piece of the leg assembly using two washers on each bolt.

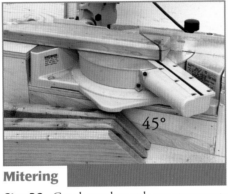

Mitering

45°

Step 20 - Cut the underneath center supports (K) to the dimensions given in the material list. Use the miter saw to cut the ends of each piece to 45 degrees.

Seats

Step 21 - Cut the seats (G) to the dimensions given in the material list. Refer to front view drawing for seat overhang. Draw a line across the seats and evenly space to screw hole locations. Countersink to a depth of ⅜". Use the screws (R) to fasten the seats to the seat supports. Plug each hole with a wooden plug, as shown in the photo inset.

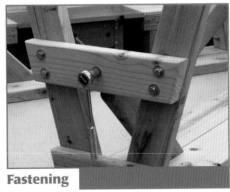

Fastening

Step 22 - Place the center supports against the leg supports and pre-drill through the leg supports into each center support. Use the lag screws (Q) to fasten center supports to leg supports.

Support Blocks

Offset

Step 23 - Cut the center support blocks (L) to the dimensions given in the material list. Lay out three screw holes into each block, two evenly spaced screw holes on the top and one screw hole centered in the side. Stagger each block and use the screws (R) to fasten blocks into position. Finish the benches and table with the Olympic Clear Wood Preservative.

Outdoor Occasional Table

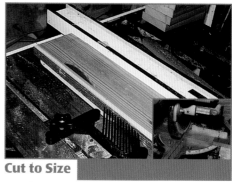

Cut to Size

Step 1 - To cut the tabletop pieces (A), plane both sides of a 16"-long piece of redwood to a thickness of 1". Joint one edge and rip the wood to a 4½" width. Crosscut the piece into six 8"-long pieces, as shown in the inset photo.

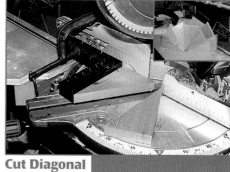

Cut Diagonal

Step 2 - Set the miter saw at a 30-degree angle. On the tabletop pieces, make a diagonal cut from corner to corner on an 8" side. Clamp a corner brace against the fence to secure the stock and keep your fingers out of the way. Stack the twelve cut pieces together to check the fit of the miter cuts, as shown in the inset. Trim, if necessary.

Remove Edge

Step 3 - Set the miter saw to a 15-degree angle. Remove an edge from the right-angle side of each tabletop piece.

Glue and Clamp

Step 4 - Using waterproof glue (F), assemble and clamp six pieces to create half of the table-top. Use a web clamp against a sturdy piece of wood scrap to apply pressure and use waxed paper (G) to make sure the glue stays on the pieces. When the glue has cured, assemble the other half. Connect the two halves using glue, the web clamp, and other clamps as needed, as shown in the photo inset.

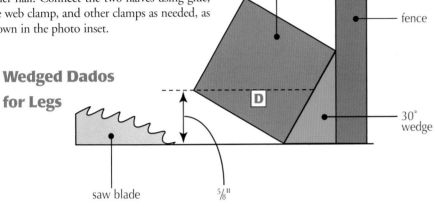

Wedged Dados for Legs

leg

fence

D

30° wedge

saw blade

$^5/_8$"

Sand Top

Step 5 - Using a belt sander, sand the outside edges of the top. Sand the top and bottom portions to achieve a flat surface.

Round Over Edges

Step 6 - Install a $^1/_8$" round-over bearing bit (H) in the router. Round the top and bottom edges of the tabletop.

Assemble Apron

Step 7 - Cut the remaining redwood for the six table apron pieces (B). Set the miter at a 30-degree angle. Trim both ends of each apron piece to form a barrel stave apron, as shown in the photo inset.

Step 8 - Using brads (I) and waterproof glue, assemble the six table apron pieces. Use scrap wood as a backing brace when nailing the ends together. Fill the nail holes and sand.

Prepare Screw Holes

Step 9 - Set the assembled and sanded apron on the underside of the tabletop. Referring to the bottom view drawing, mark the screw hole mounting locations. Plan on installing one screw in each segment of the tabletop.

Step 10 - For each screw, countersink a $^3/_8$" hole 1"-deep in the bottom edge of the apron, as shown in the photo inset.

Material List	Wood	Quantity	T x W x L
A table top pieces	redwood	6	1" x 4$^1/_2$" x 8"
B table apron	redwood	6	1" x 1$^3/_4$" x 6$^3/_4$"
C shelf triangle	redwood		1" x 13" x 13"
D legs	maple	3	1$^1/_4$" x 1$^1/_4$" x 14"
E support block	maple		1" x 1$^1/_4$" x 1$^3/_4$"
Supply List			
F waterproof glue			
G waxed paper			
H round-over bearing bit			$^1/_8$"
I brads			
J apron screws		12	1$^1/_2$"
K round-over router bit			$^1/_8$"
L leg screws		10	1$^1/_2$"
M doweling rod	cherry		$^3/_8$" diam.
N spray-on Spar polyurethane			

Bottom View

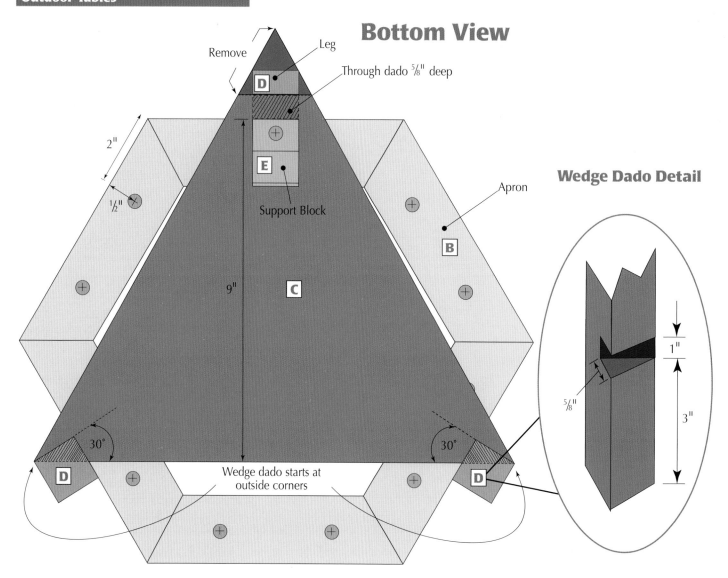

Remove

Leg

Through dado ⅝" deep

D

2"

½"

E

Support Block

9"

C

Apron

B

30°   30°

D   D

Wedge dado starts at
outside corners

Wedge Dado Detail

1"

⅝"

3"

Attach Top to Apron

Step 11 - Apply waterproof glue to the edge of the apron that mates to the bottom of the table, center the apron on the table, and install twelve apron screws (J), one screw in each tabletop segment.

Step 12 - Cut and glue up enough redwood to form a 13" x 13" x 13" triangle for the shelf (C).

Check Placement

Step 13 - Cut the legs (D) to the dimensions given in the material list. Use a ⅛" round-over bit (K) to rout the edges of the legs.

Step 14 - Temporarily clamp the legs on the apron. Set the assembly on top of the shelf to ensure the proper placement of the legs on the shelf.

Cut Dados

Step 15 - When the legs fit against the apron and shelf, cut 1"-wide dados for the shelf. Two of the legs have a wedge cut; the remaining leg has a through cut. All dados start 3" up from the bottom of the legs. Set the table saw up with 1" stacked dado blades, ⅝"-high. The wedge dados are cut by laying a 30-degree angle wedge piece against the saw fence to achieve the proper angle (refer to the wedged dado detail). The wedge dado starts at the outside corner of each of the two legs and should come out midway through the thickness of the legs. Cut the through dado ⅝"-deep on the remaining leg.

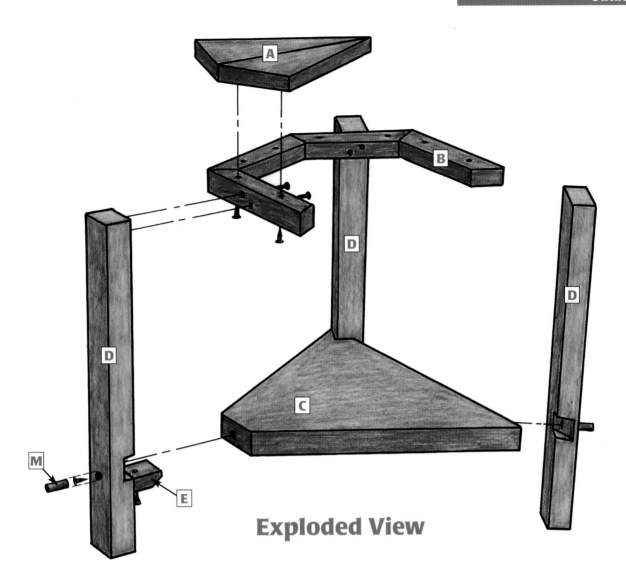

Exploded View

Drill Holes

Step 16 - Drill a ⅜" countersink hole, 1"-deep on the outside of each leg, across from where it mates with the shelf. Then drill two ⅜" countersink holes on the inside of the apron across from each leg location.

Step 17 - Attach the legs to the apron and shelf using waterproof glue (F) and the 1½" leg screws (L). Use two screws per leg on the apron inside and one on each outside shelf location. Use enough clamps to be certain that the assembly stays square.

Attach Support Block

Step 18 - Because of the short grain on the one edge of the shelf triangle, add a support block (E) on the bottom of the shelf using wood glue and a screw.

Fill Holes

Step 19 - Use pieces of ⅜" cherry doweling rod (M) to fill the countersunk holes on the outside legs. Glue, saw flush, and sand.

Step 20 - Because this table is designed to be used outdoors, apply four coats of spray-on Spar polyurethane (N) after the final sanding.

Chaise Lounge

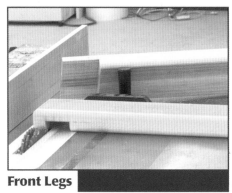

Front Legs

Step 1 - Cut all pieces to the dimensions given in the material list. Label each piece appropriately.

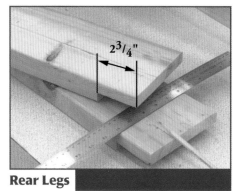

2³/₄"

Rear Legs

Step 2 - The front legs (D) and back legs (E) are half lapped over the sides (A) in final assembly. Use the table saw with a ¾" stacked dado blade raised to a height of ¾" and the fence moved away from the blade 2". Start by passing each blank through the blade and then nibble away the material until you reach the ends, as shown in Steps 1 and 2.

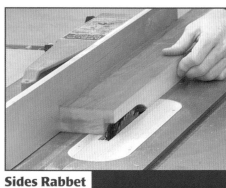

Sides Rabbet

Step 3 - A rabbet is milled along the entire top inside edge of the two side blanks (A). Adjust the fence to 2¾" away from dado blade and leave the height the same as in Step 2. Pass each side blank through the blade.

Axle Cover

Step 4 - A ½" groove is milled down the center of the axle cover (O). Use the table saw with the dado blade raised to a height of ½" to make the groove. To center the groove on the axle cover, flip the piece end for end and run the cover through the blade again.

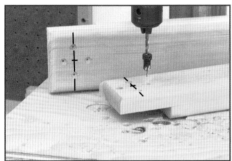

Front Legs

Step 5 - Fasten the legs to the sides with screws. Use the drill press with a #6 countersinking bit to pre-drill into the legs. Use four wood screws (X) for each leg. Lay out a diamond shape for screw locations.

Rear Legs

Step 6 - The rear legs get fastened to the sides with the wood screws (X). Refer to side view drawing for screw layout pattern. Use the countersinking bit to pre-drill the seven screw holes in each leg.

Material List

		Wood	Quantity	T x W x L
A	sides*	redwood	2	1½" x 3½" x 84"
B	slats	redwood	18	¾" x 3½" x 22"
C	front leg brace	redwood	1	1½" x 3½" x 19"
D	front legs	redwood	2	1½" x 3½" x 16"
E	back legs	redwood	2	1½" x 5½" x 13½"
F	armrests	redwood	2	1½" x 3½" x 12"
G	armrest supports	redwood	4	1½" x 3½" x 12"
H	back supports	redwood	2	1½" x 2¾" x 27½"
I	back support slat	redwood	1	¾" x 3½" x 20½"
J	rear platform brace	redwood	1	1½" x 5½" x 19"
K	platform stop blocks	redwood	2	1½" x 1½" x 19"
L	swing arms*	redwood	2	1½" x 1½" x 17"
M	swing arm rail	redwood	1	1½" x 1½" x 8¾"
N	rear cover plate	redwood	1	¾" x 3½" x 23½"
O	axle cover	redwood	1	1½" x 1½" x 19"
P	rear end brace	redwood	1	1½" x 3½" x 20½"

Supply List

			Quantity	
Q	bolts with nuts for swing arms		2	⅜" x 4"
R	washers for swing arms		4	1" diam. x ⅜"
S	washers for swing arms		2	1½" diam. x ⅜"
T	lock washers for swing arms		2	¹¹⁄₁₆" diam. x ⅜"
U	washers for axle		4	1½" diam. x ½"
V	all thread axle w/nuts		1	½" diam. x 3'
W	solid stainless steel rod		1	½" diam. x 22"
X	wood screws exterior			#7 x 1⅝"
Y	wood screws exterior			#8 x 2½"
Z	double-sided tape			
AA	wooden plugs			
BB	wagon wheels			10"

*Patterns needed for this project are located in pattern packet.

Axle Hole

Step 7 - A ½" through hole is centered and drilled into each rear leg for the axle. Refer to the side view drawing for the hole locations.

Pre-Drilling

Step 8 - The three pre-drilled holes in the outside face of each leg are for the screws that fasten the rear platform brace (J). Refer to the side view drawing for screw locations. Use the drill press and the countersinking bit to make the holes.

Handle Pattern

Step 9 - Locate the pattern for the handle in the pattern packet. Adhere it to the ends of each side blank (A) with the curve toward the bottom edge and the top flush with the rabbet on the inside, as shown in the photo inset. Use the band saw to mill each profile.

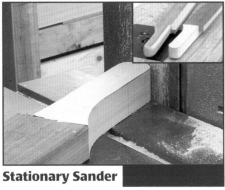

Stationary Sander

Step 10 - Use the sander to round the ends. Use the router with a ½" round-over bit to ease the edges of the sides. Route all edges on both sides except the top inside long edge and the two rear ends, as shown in the photo inset.

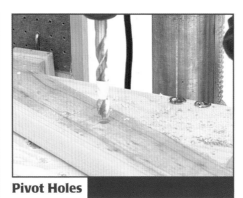

Pivot Holes

Step 11 - Locate the pivot holes in the sides for the back supports by referring to the side view drawing. Use the drill press with a ½" drill bit and the depth stop set at ¾" to make each hole into the sides.

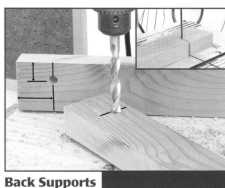

Back Supports

Step 12 - The two holes in the back supports (H) are for the solid steel rod (W). Measure down from the top of each blank 1" and in from the end 2". Use the drill press with a ½" drill bit to make the two through holes. Notch the opposite end's bottom edge to fit around the rear end brace, as shown in the photo inset.

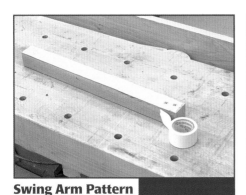

Swing Arm Pattern

Step 13 - Locate the swing arm pattern in the pattern packet and adhere using double-sided tape (Z) one to each arm.

Milling Swing Arms

Step 14 - Located on the pattern are three milling operations. Start by first sanding one end to make the point. Then drill the through holes located on the opposite end with the drill press and a ⅜" bit, as shown in the top right photo inset. And finally pre-drill for the two screws on the pointed end with the #6 countersinking bit, as shown in the bottom right photo inset.

Swing Arm Rail

Step 15 - The swing arm rail is attached to the swing arms with the wood screws (Y). Align the arms so that the point is flush with the work bench and also the rail. Pre-drill into the rail through the holes in the arms. Fasten each arm into position.

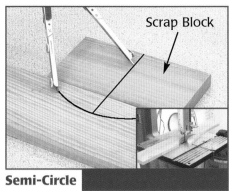

Semi-Circle

Step 16 - The rear cover plate (N) receives a semi-circle centered on the top edge to allow a hand to slip in and raise the back rest when the back rest is in the down position. Use a compass to make a 5" radius to a depth of 1¼". Use the band saw to mill the semi-circle, as shown in the photo inset.

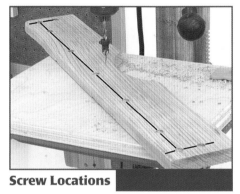

Screw Locations

Step 17 - Measure up from the bottom edge of the rear cover plate ¾" and evenly space seven screw locations. Two screw locations are milled into the ends of the cover plate. Use the drill press with the #6 countersinking bit to pre-drill deep enough for the wood plugs (AA).

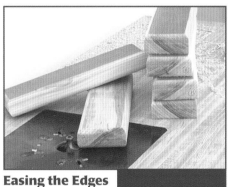

Easing the Edges

Step 18 - Ease the face edges of the armrest supports (G) and all edges of the armrest (F) with the router table and a ½" round-over bit.

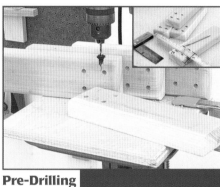

Pre-Drilling

Step 19 - Each armrest support is fastened to the sides with the wood screws (Y). Refer to the side view drawing for the four screw locations and mark these on each armrest support, as shown in the photo inset. Use the drill press with the countersinking bit to pre-drill each location deep enough for the wooden plugs (AA).

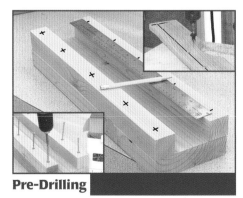

Pre-Drilling

Step 20 - Evenly space five screw hole locations in the two platform stop blocks (K) and use the drill press to pre-drill, as shown in the main photo and the top photo inset. Fasten the stop blocks to the rear platform brace (I) using the wood screws (Y), as shown in the bottom photo inset.

Rear Leg Assembly

Step 21 - Fasten the two rear legs to the rear platform brace with the wood screws (Y). Refer to the side view drawing for the platform brace location. Use a drill to first pre-drill into the platform, then screw the legs into position. Attach the rear legs to the inside edge of the sides with the wood screws (X), as shown in the photo inset. Refer to the side view drawing for rear leg locations.

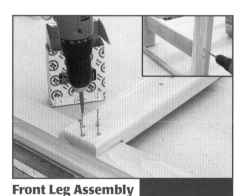

Front Leg Assembly

Step 22 - Refer to the side view drawing for front leg and front leg brace locations. Attach legs to the inside edge of the sides with the wood screws (X). Pre-drill for wooden plugs and attach the front leg brace (C) to the legs with the wood screws (Y), as shown in the photo inset.

Side view

Back Rest Detail

Back Leg Detail

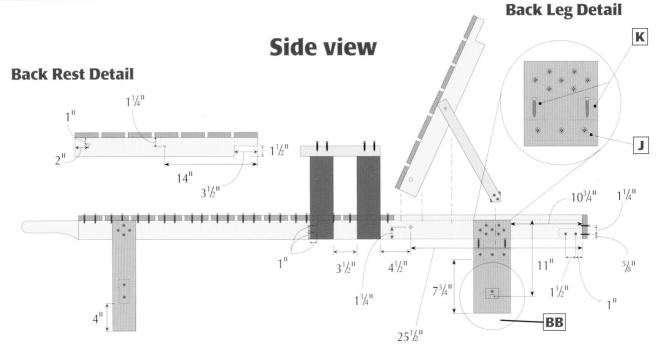

$1\frac{1}{4}''$

$1''$

$2''$

$1\frac{1}{2}''$

$14''$

$3\frac{1}{2}''$

K

J

$10\frac{3}{4}''$ $1\frac{1}{4}''$

$1''$

$3\frac{1}{2}''$ $4\frac{1}{2}''$

$11''$

$1\frac{3}{4}''$

$7\frac{3}{4}''$

$1\frac{1}{2}''$

$1''$

$\frac{5}{8}''$

$4''$

BB

$25\frac{1}{2}''$

Back Supports

Step 23 - The steel rod (W) acts as a hinge for the back rest section. Feed the rod through both back supports and into the holes drilled into the sides. Place the back supports 3" away from the sides. Refer to the exploded view drawing for the proper orientation.

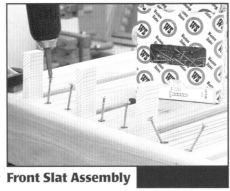

Front Slat Assembly

Step 24 - The slats (B) are separated by a ½". Dry-fit all slats on the front section of the lounge. Start by the handles in the sides and work your way back. Use ½" spacers and fasten the slats to the sides with the wood screws (X). Refer to the side view drawing for orientation.

Back Rest Slats

Step 25 - Clamp the smaller first slat (I) on the back supports flush with the ends. Swing back supports up to check for clearance from the sides and opposite slat. Make any adjustments necessary to allow a smooth motion. Fasten all slats with the wood screws (X) maintaining a ½" space.

Bolt Locations

Step 26 - Use bolts to fasten the swing arms to the back supports. Refer to the side view drawing for the two bolt hole locations. Use a drill with a ⅜" bit to make each hole.

Swing Arm Assembly

Step 27 - Use the bolts with nuts (Q), washers (R, S), and lock washers (T) to connect the swing arm to the back supports.

Arm Supports

Step 28 - Refer to the side view drawing for armrest support locations. Use the wood screws (Y) to fasten each armrest, as shown in photo BB. After fastening the armrest closest to the back, measure forward 3½" and fasten the second armrest support.

Armrests

Step 29 - Place the armrest centered on top of the supports with the back end flush with the back armrest support. Lay out the four hole locations. Use the drill press to countersink for wood plugs, as shown in the photo inset. Use the wood screws (Y) to fasten armrest to armrest supports.

Pre-Drilling

Step 30 - The rear end brace (P) is fastened to the sides with two wood screws (Y). Refer to the side view drawing for screw hole locations. Pre-drill into the sides for wood plugs. Screw the rear end brace in place, making sure the bottom edge is flush with the bottom edge of the sides and the side edge of the brace is flush with the ends of the sides. Lower the back rest to check the fit and make any adjustments necessary to allow for a smooth transition.

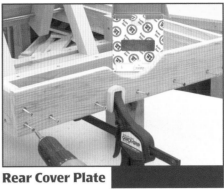

Rear Cover Plate

Step 31 - Screw the rear cover plate to the sides and rear end brace with the wood screws (X).

Pre-Drilling

Step 32 - The axle cover is fastened to the rear legs with the wood screws (Y). Measure up ¾" from the center of the axle hole. Pre-drill using the countersinking bit.

Axle Cover Assembly

Step 33 - Place the axle through the holes and place the axle cover over the axle. Pre-drill into the axle cover through the holes in the rear legs. Use the wood screws (Y) to fasten the axle cover in place.

Wheel Assembly

Step 34 - Slide the axle through the holes of the rear legs and place a washer (U) between the rear leg and wheel. Place the remaining washer on the outside of the wheel. Tighten the two nuts. Determine the final length of the axle and cut. Protect the chaise with a waterproof finish.

Exploded view

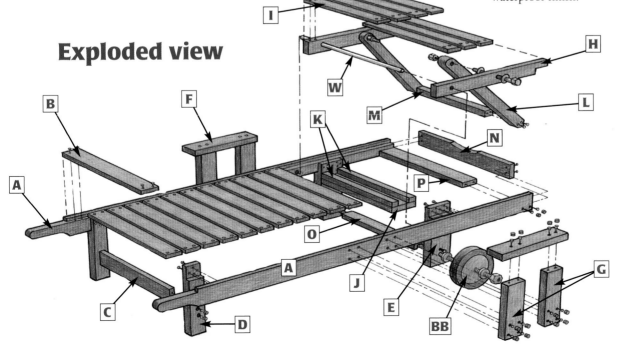

Adirondack Chair

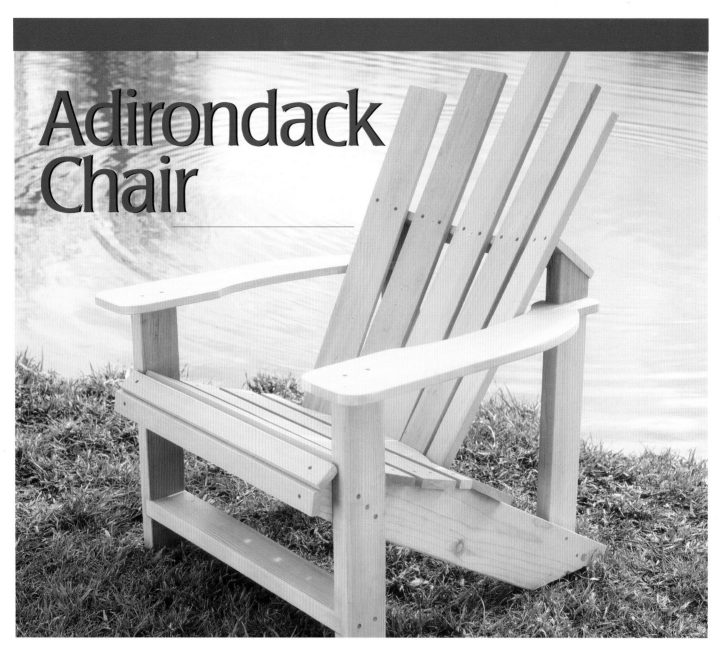

Rear Legs

Step 1 - You will need the six patterns from the pattern packet. Cut the back legs (B) to the dimensions given in the material list. Using double-sided tape (Q), place the pattern onto one of the back leg blanks. Use the band saw to cut out the profile. Trace the pattern onto the second leg and repeat the process.

Making Dadoes

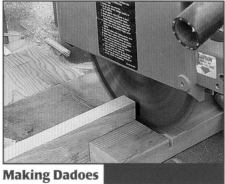

Step 2 - Cut the front legs (A) to the dimensions given in the material list. The legs receive 1½"-wide x ¾"-deep dadoes on the lower inside area. These dadoes will later house the stretcher. Refer to the side view drawing for the locations of the dadoes. To make the dadoes, mark their locations and use the radial arm saw.

Pre-Drilling

Step 3 - Cut the stretcher (C) to the dimensions given in the material list. The stretcher is fastened into the dadoes that were just milled into the legs. Refer to the drawings for screw locations. Pre-drill into the sides of the legs first before screwing in the #6 x 2½" wood screws (N).

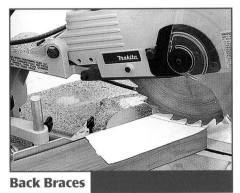

Back Braces

Step 4 - Back braces (E) are fastened to the lower inside portion of the back legs. The upper support blank gets fastened to the top portion of the back braces. Cut the back braces to the dimensions given in the material list. Attach the pattern from the pattern packet to the top edge of one back brace blank. Use the miter saw to make the angled cut. Trace the angle to the other blank and repeat.

Frame Assembly

Step 5 - It's now time for partial assembly. With the stretcher already attached to the front legs, attach the back legs to the front legs. Refer to the side view drawing for the location where front legs and back legs meet. Before fastening, be sure that the back legs sit flush with the level ground. Clamp the legs in place. Use #6 x 2½" wood screws to fasten the legs together. The back braces are fastened to the inside portion of the back legs. Refer to the side view drawing for back brace locations and the location of the #6 x 2½" wood screws.

Material List		Wood	Quantity	T x W x L
A	front legs	redwood	2	1½" x 3½" x 22½"
B	back legs*	redwood	2	1½" x 5½" x 36"
C	stretcher	redwood		1½" x 3½" x 25½"
D	arms*	redwood	2	¾" x 7¾" x 30"
E	back braces*	redwood	2	1½" x 3½" x 26¼"
F	upper support*	redwood		¾" x 5½" x 21"
G	lower support*	redwood		¾" x 4¼" x 25½"
H	rear seat slat*	redwood		¾" x 4" x 25½"
I	seat slats	redwood	2	¾" x 3½" x 25½"
J	seat slat	redwood		¾" x 3" x 24"
K	seat slats (front)	redwood	2	¾" x 1¾" x 25½"
L	back slats (outside)	redwood	2	¾" x 3½" x 30"
M	back slats (inside)	redwood	2	¾" x 3½" x 33"
N	back slat (middle)	redwood		¾" x 3½" x 36"
Supply List				
O	wood screws			#6 x 2½"
P	wood screws			#6 x 1¼"
Q	brads			1"
R	double-sided tape			

* Patterns needed for this project are located in pattern packet.

Arms

Step 6 - Cut the arms (D) to the dimensions given in the material list. Attach the arm pattern to the top of one arm blank using double-sided tape. Cut the profile using the band saw, staying just outside the line. Trace the pattern on the other arm blank, and repeat the process. Clean up the cut using a drum sander.

Upper Support

Step 7 - Cut the upper support bracket (F) to the dimensions given in the material list. Attach the pattern and use the band saw to cut the profile, making sure to stay on the outer portion of the lines. Clean up the cut using a drum sander.

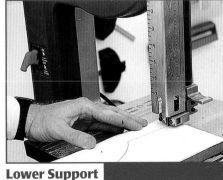

Lower Support

Step 8 - Cut the lower support bracket (G) to the dimensions given in the material list. With the pattern attached, cut the profile using the band saw.

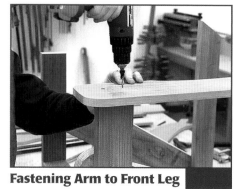

Fastening Arm to Front Leg

Step 9 - With the frame assembled, as shown in Step 5, fasten the arms to the front legs. For the location of the arms, refer to the front view drawing. Fasten the fronts of the arms in the proper location using #6 x 1¼" wood screws (P); the back portions of the arms are then attached to the back braces. Be sure each arm is in a level position before attaching it to the back braces. Pre-drill from the insides of the back braces into the arms before fastening them with #6 x 2½" wood screws.

Fastening Arm to Back Braces

Step 10 - As we built this Adirondack chair using kiln-dried redwood, we found ourselves splitting a few pieces. So we highly recommend pre-drilling every screw placement. It takes a little more time, but it also saves you from going back and forth to the lumberyard. We have found that using a few brads (Q) to hold (tack) the blanks in position makes pre-drilling much easier.

Tacking

Step 11 - Tacking is illustrated here on the lower support. Refer to the side view drawing for the location of the lower support bracket. Once it is tacked in position, evenly space two of the #6 x 1¼" wood screws on both sides of the lower support blank and fasten it to the back legs.

Upper Support Assembly

Step 12 - The upper support bracket is used to support the back slats. Tack the upper support blank on the top edges of the back braces and pre-drill. Fasten the upper support bracket to the back braces with the #6 x 1¼" wood screws. Refer to the side view drawing for the orientation and placement of the upper support blank.

Back Slats

Step 13 - Cut the back slats (L, M, N) to the dimensions given in the material list. When tacking down the back slats, start by first centering the middle back slat on both the upper and lower supports. Evenly space the remaining four slats in a fan profile. Refer to the front view drawing for the proper orientation of the back slats. Pre-drill through the slats and into the supports. Fasten with the #6 x 1¼" wood screws.

Seat Slats

Step 14 - Cut the rear seat slat (H) to the dimensions given in the material list. Attach the pattern from the pattern packet to the rear seat slat blank. Use the band saw and cut the profile, staying just outside the lines. Clean up the cut using a drum sander. Place and center the rear seat slat on the back legs next to the back slats. Fasten the slats to the back legs using the #6 x 1¼" wood screws.

Step 15 - Cut the two seat slats (I) to the dimensions given in the material list. Place and fasten these blanks on the back legs. Fasten the blanks to the back legs using the #6 x 1¼" wood screws. Refer to the side view drawing for the proper spacing between seat slats.

Side View

Front View

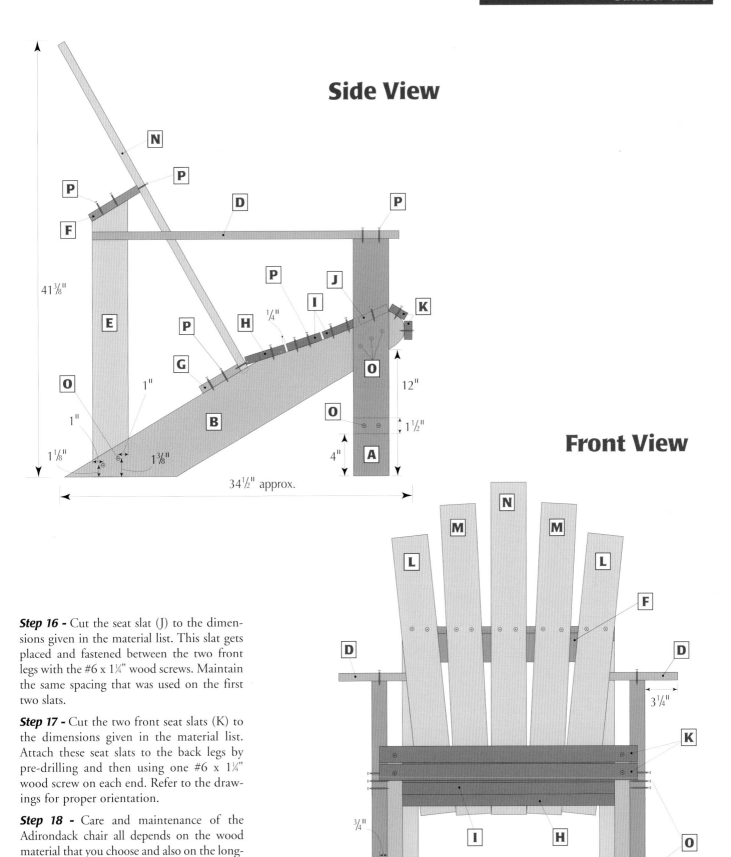

Step 16 - Cut the seat slat (J) to the dimensions given in the material list. This slat gets placed and fastened between the two front legs with the #6 x 1¼" wood screws. Maintain the same spacing that was used on the first two slats.

Step 17 - Cut the two front seat slats (K) to the dimensions given in the material list. Attach these seat slats to the back legs by pre-drilling and then using one #6 x 1¼" wood screw on each end. Refer to the drawings for proper orientation.

Step 18 - Care and maintenance of the Adirondack chair all depends on the wood material that you choose and also on the long-term look you are trying to achieve. When redwood is set outside with no preservative to protect it against the elements, it will turn gray over time, taking on a very weathered and aged look. Some people just love that look. Others want to keep the new redwood look; for these people we recommend using weather-proofing oil.

Summer's Breeze Porch Swing

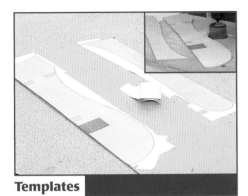

Templates

Step 1 - Cut the back supports (A) and seat supports (B) to the dimensions given in the material list. Locate the back support and seat support patterns in the pattern packet and adhere to each blank. (We made masonite templates of each pattern to make multiple swings; however, this step is optional.)

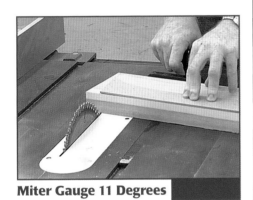

Miter Gauge 11 Degrees

Step 2 - Cut one end of each back support to 11 degrees. Use the table saw and miter gauge to make the cuts. Be sure to save your off-cuts for glue-ups later.

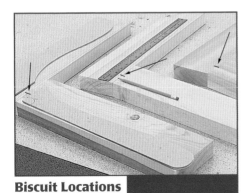

Biscuit Locations

Step 3 - Lay out and align each back support and seat support. Mark the center where the two blanks meet for the #20 biscuit (P) locations.

Material List	Wood	Quantity	T x W x L
Body			
A back supports*	pine	3	$1\frac{1}{2}$" x 4" x $19\frac{1}{2}$"
B seat supports*	pine	3	$1\frac{1}{2}$" x 4" x $21\frac{1}{4}$"
C bottom cross support	pine	1	$1\frac{1}{2}$" x 4" x 60"
D seat slats	pine	20	$\frac{3}{4}$" x $1\frac{3}{4}$" x 48"
E armrests*	pine	2	$1\frac{1}{2}$" x $3\frac{1}{2}$" x $20\frac{3}{4}$"
F armrest supports*	pine	2	$1\frac{1}{2}$" x $3\frac{1}{2}$" x $13\frac{3}{4}$"
G back-side joint braces	pine	4	$\frac{3}{4}$" x $1\frac{1}{2}$" x 6"
Supply List			
H eye bolts w/washers & nuts		2	6" long
I eye bolts w/washers & nuts		2	$6\frac{1}{2}$" long
J w.s.** seat slats to back/seat supports		60	#6 x $1\frac{5}{8}$"
K w.s.** arm supports to cross support		6	#8 x $2\frac{1}{2}$"
L w.s.** back support to arm rest		4	#8 x $2\frac{1}{2}$"
M w.s.** arm rest to arm support		4	#8 x $2\frac{1}{2}$"
N w.s.** seat supports to cross supports		3	#8 x $2\frac{1}{2}$"
O w.s.** seat supports to arm supports		4	#8 x $2\frac{1}{2}$"
P biscuits		6	#20
Q double-sided tape			
R spray paint		(4-5 cans)	blossom white

* Patterns needed for this project are located in the pattern packet.
Each porch and mounting will vary; chain and mounting hardware is required
** w.s. = wood screw

Side View

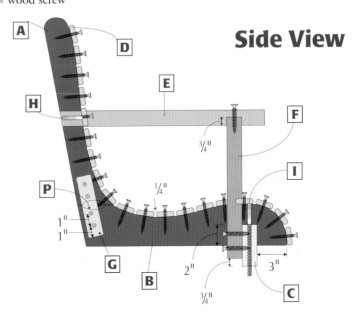

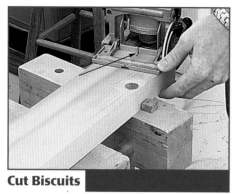

Cut Biscuits

Step 4 - With the biscuit joiner, make two slots in each seat support and back support. Each slot should be centered and in from the side edges ⅜".

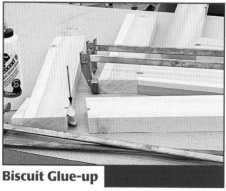

Biscuit Glue-up

Step 5 - Place glue inside each biscuit slot and where the two blanks meet. Insert each biscuit and clamp the two blanks together. Use the off-cuts in step 2 to help in the clamping process.

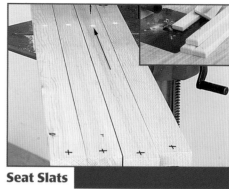

Seat Slats

Step 6 - Cut the seat slats (D) to the dimensions given in the material list. Locate the three holes for each slat in the front view drawing. Use the drill press with a countersinking bit to drill the holes. Use a ¼" round-over bit to ease the top edges of each slat, as shown in the photo inset.

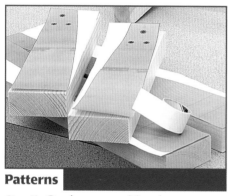

Patterns

Step 7 - Cut the armrests (E) and arm supports (F) to the dimensions given in the material list. Locate the arm support and armrest patterns in the pattern packet and adhere to each blank. (Make copies of each pattern as shown or trace pattern to remaining blanks.)

Armrests

Step 8 - Transfer each dado line down the side of each blank for the start and stop locations. Make a dado on the bottom side of each armrest using the table saw and miter gauge with a stacked dado blade raised to a height of ¾".

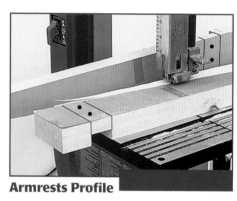

Armrests Profile

Step 9 - Each armrest is cut out using the band saw by just freehanding each blank through the blade trying to stay outside the line. Use the drum sander to clean up saw marks and to sand smooth to the lines, as shown in the photo inset.

Front View

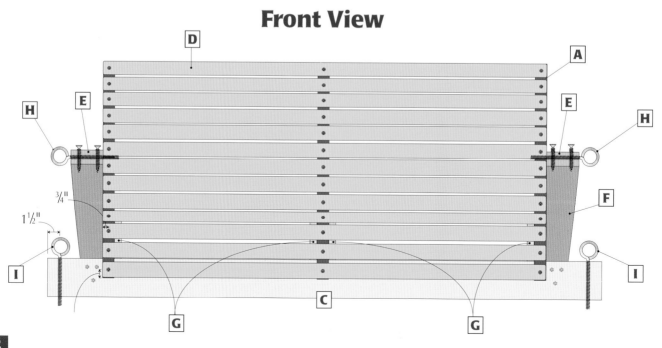

Rest Supports

Step 10 - Use the band saw to cut the arm support profiles. Use the drum sander to smooth the cuts, as shown in the photo inset.

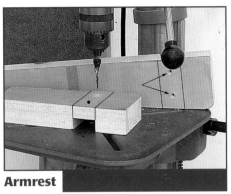

Armrest

Step 11 - Two holes are drilled and countersunk into each armrest. Use the drill press with a #6 countersinking bit to drill the holes. A slight roundover is milled on the top edges of each armrest, as shown in the photo inset.

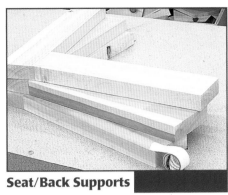

Seat/Back Supports

Step 12 - Gang the three seat and back supports together using double-sided tape.

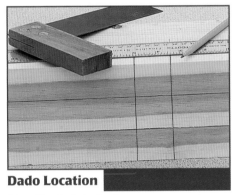

Dado Location

Step 13 - A dado in the seat supports houses the bottom cross support (C). Locate the dado location from the side view drawing. Transfer the location to the ganged supports.

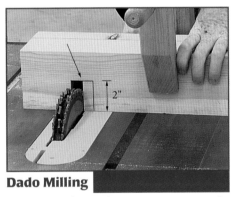

Dado Milling

Step 14 - Clamp the seat supports to the miter gauge on the table saw. Raise the stacked dado blade to a height of 2" and pass the supports through the blade making a couple of passes.

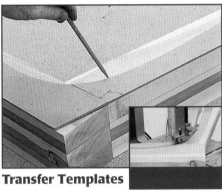

Transfer Templates

Step 15 - Separate the ganged supports. If using templates, transfer each profile onto each support or make copies of the patterns and adhere them to each support. Use the band saw to cut each profile out, as shown in the photo inset, and drum sand to smooth the cut.

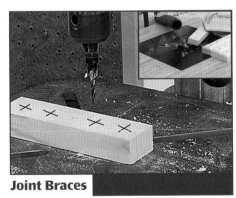

Joint Braces

Step 16 - Cut the back-side joint braces (G) to the dimensions given in the material list. Refer to the back view support drawing for the four screw locations. Transfer locations and countersink using the drill press. A slight round-over is milled to the top edges of each brace, as shown in the photo inset.

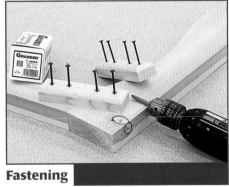

Fastening

Step 17 - The purpose of the braces is to strengthen the joint on each seat and back support. The center support receives two braces on both sides, and each end support receives one brace on its inside surface. Stagger the screws on the inside support to allow room for all screws. Screw braces in place.

Eye Bolt Locations

Step 18 - Cut the bottom cross brace (C) to the dimensions given in the material list. Each end of the cross brace receives ⅜" through holes for the eye bolts (I). Refer to the front view drawing for eye bolt locations. Use drill press to drill holes.

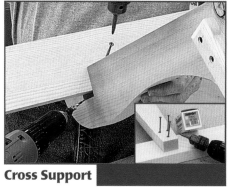

Cross Support

Step 19 - Locate the armrest support locations from the front view drawing and fasten to the inside surface of the cross brace using the wood screws (K), as shown in the photo inset. Center the seat/back support onto the cross support. Toe screw with the wood screw (N) through the seat/back support into the cross support.

Step 20 - The two end supports sit flush against the armrest supports. Fasten the two end seat/back supports to the cross support by repeating step 19.

Fastening Armrests

Step 21 - Place the two armrests onto the armrest supports. Use a level and level the armrest. Mark and drill ⅜" through holes where back of armrest meets the end back supports. Fasten the armrest to the arm support with the wood screws (M), as shown in the photo inset.

Support Screws

Step 22 - From the inside of the two end seat/back supports, two screws (L) get screwed into the armrest for added strength.

Seat Slat Locations

Step 23 - The two end seat/back supports are also fastened to the armrest support from the inside with the wood screws (O).

Step 24 - Fasten the seat slats to the seat/back supports with the wood screws (J). Start the first seat slat on the bottom edge of the seat/back supports, and space each slat with a ¼" spacer.

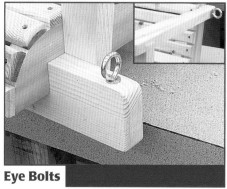

Eye Bolts

Step 25 - The eye bolts (I) get placed in the cross brace. The eye bolts (H) are placed into the armrest and back support, as shown in the photo inset. Paint with spray cans (R).

Back View

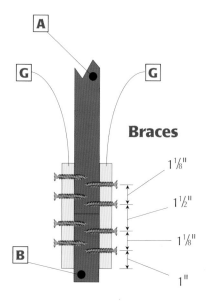

Braces

A

G   G

1⅛"

1½"

1⅛"

B

1"

Garden Bench

Cut Posts

Step 1 - Using the radial arm saw cut the front and back posts (A, B) to the lengths given in the material list.

Step 2 - Cut the side frames (C), front frame (D), and back frame (E) to the lengths given in the material list.

Frame Placement

Step 3 - Referring to the side view drawing, measure 9" up from the bottom of the front and back posts and ¾" in from the inside edges. Mark a line for the side frame placement.

Material List

		Wood	Quantity	T x W x L
A	back posts	redwood	2	4" x 4" x 30"
B	front posts	redwood	2	4" x 4" x 22"
C	side frames	redwood	2	1½" x 3½" x 16"
D	front frame	redwood	1	¾" x 3½" x 32"
E	back frame	redwood	1	¾" x 3½" x 32"
F	back supports	redwood	2	¾" x 3½" x 38"
G	seat slats	redwood	3	¾" x 3½" x 39⅜"
H	seat slat	redwood	1	¾" x 3½" x 32"
I	back slats	redwood	2	¾" x 3½" x 18"
J	back slats	redwood	2	¾" x 3½" x 19"
K	back slats	redwood	2	¾" x 3½" x 20"
L	back slat	redwood	1	¾" x 3½" x 21"
M	arm braces	redwood	2	1½" x 1½" x 4½"
N	arms	redwood	2	¾" x 5½" x 19"

Supply List

O	wood screws			#8 x 2"
P	wood screws			#6 x 1¼", 1⅝", 2"
Q	post caps	(cedar)	2	4" x 4"
R	Liquid Nails adhesive			
S	Superdeck exterior semi-transparent stain (coastal grey)			
T	Metal Effects metallic paint (copper), patina (blue)*			

*This item is available from CPC, Modern Masters Inc.
For more information call (800) 942-3166

Pre-Drill

Step 4 - Mark the side frame pieces as shown in the front view drawing. Pre-drill.

Attach Side Frame

Step 5 - Using the wood screws (O), attach the side frame pieces to the front and back posts, allowing ¾" from the front edge for the front frame.

Front and Back Frame

Step 6 - Pre-drill the front and back frame pieces. Refer to the front view drawing for the placement of the screws. Using the 1⅝" wood screws (P), attach the front and back blanks to the side frame ends.

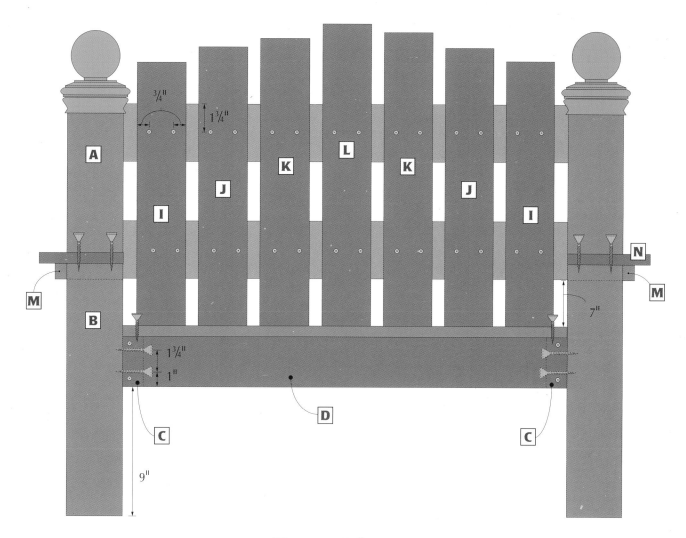

3/4"

1 3/4"

A

I

J

K

L

K

J

I

N

M

M

7"

B

1 3/4"

1"

C

9"

D

C

Front View

Back Supports

Step 7 - Cut the back supports (F) to the length given in the material list. Measure up ¾" from the top and bottom edges and 1½" in from the side edge. Mark and pre-drill. Refer to the side view drawing for locations of the back supports. Using the 1⅝" wood screws (P), screw the back supports into place.

Side View

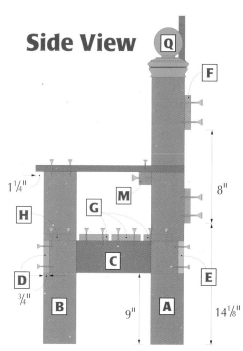

Q

F

1¼"

8"

H

G

M

D

C

¾"

B

A

E

9"

14⅛"

Mark Seat Notch

Step 8 - Cut the seat slats (G, H) to the lengths given in the material list. Lay out the seat slats using a ⅜"-wide spacer between slats. Measure and mark for the notch around the back post.

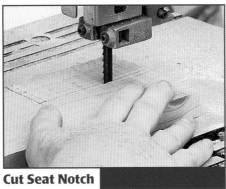

Cut Seat Notch

Step 9 - Cut along the lines using a band saw.

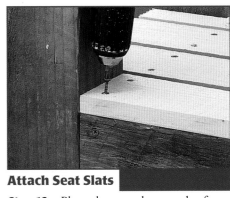

Attach Seat Slats

Step 10 - Place the seat slats on the frame using the ⅜"-wide spacer between the slats. For the screw locations, measure in ¾" from the post's inside edge, pre-drill, and screw the slats to the frame using the 1⅝" wood screws (P).

Attach Back Slats

Step 11 - Cut the back slats (I, J, K, L) to the lengths given in the material list. Referring to the front drawing for screw placement, pre-drill and screw slats to the back support using 1¼" wood screws (P) using a ¾" spacer between the slats.

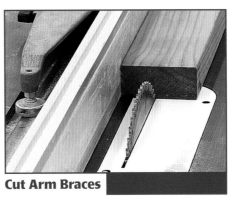

Cut Arm Braces

Step 12 - Using the table saw, cut the arm braces (M) to the dimensions given in the material list.

Attach Brace

Step 13 - Measure 7" up from the seat on the back post for the arm brace placement. Keep the inside edges of the post and brace even. Using 2½" wood screws (P), pre-drill and screw the arm brace to the post.

Cut Arm

Step 14 - Cut the arms (N) to the dimensions given in the material list. Using a band saw, measure and cut a notch to fit around the back posts on the arms.

Attach Arms

Step 15 - For the placement of the screws to attach the arms, measure and mark 1¼" from the inside edge, and 2¼" and 4¼" from the front edge of the arm. Repeat, but mark 2" on center from the first marks for the remaining screw placements, as shown in the inset photo. Pre-drill and screw the arm to the arm brace using 1¼" wood screws (P) and the 1⅝" wood screws (P) for the front of the arm into the post.

Finish

Step 16 - Sand all edges lightly. Glue the post caps to the posts using Liquid Nails adhesive (R).

Step 17 - Finish as desired. We used a gray exterior deck stain for the bench and copper paint and blue patina for the post caps.

Garden Obelisk

Leg Angles

Step 1 - Cut the legs (A) to the dimensions given in the material list.

Step 2 - Set the table saw blade to an 8-degree angle and set a miter gauge to an 8-degree angle from the right of 90 degrees. To find your 0-degree cutting edge, line up a straight edge with the blade and make a line, as shown in the inset photo.

Step 3 - With the miter gauge set to the left of the blade, cut one end of each leg.

Reverse Cut

Step 4 - Move the miter gauge to the right groove. Keep each piece oriented the same as the previous step. Line up the opposite end of the leg with the inside edge of the blade. Cut each leg piece.

Cut Legs

Step 5 - Straighten the table saw blade to 90 degrees and move the fence to the right of the blade 1½". Cut one leg.

Step 6 - Run the wider half of the just-cut leg through the blade again. You should get two legs out of one board. Repeat with a second leg for four legs.

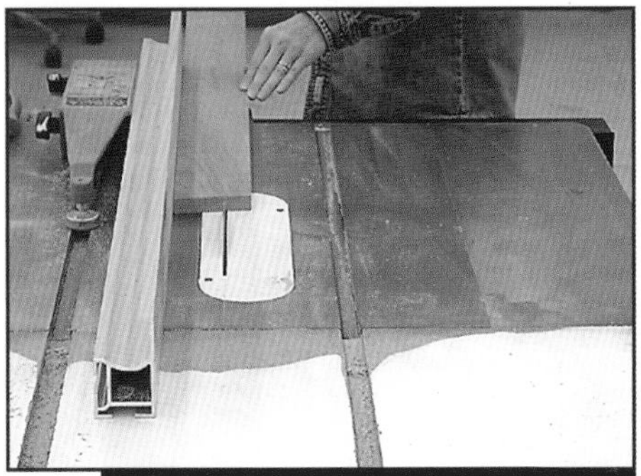

Legs

Step 7 - Set the fence 2⅛" from the blade and rip the remaining four legs to 2⅛".

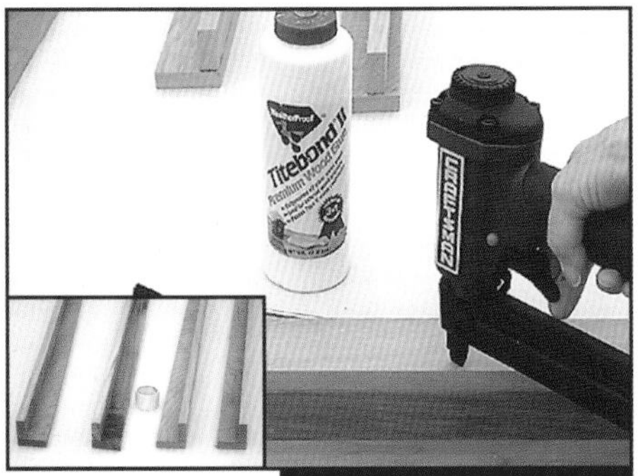

Assemble Legs

Step 8 - Dry-fit the legs together, matching one 1½" leg to one 2⅛" leg. There should be two of each orientation, as shown in the photo inset. It might help to use double-sided tape. Make sure that all angles match.

Step 9 - Use wood glue and evenly spaced brads (P) to form the corner legs.

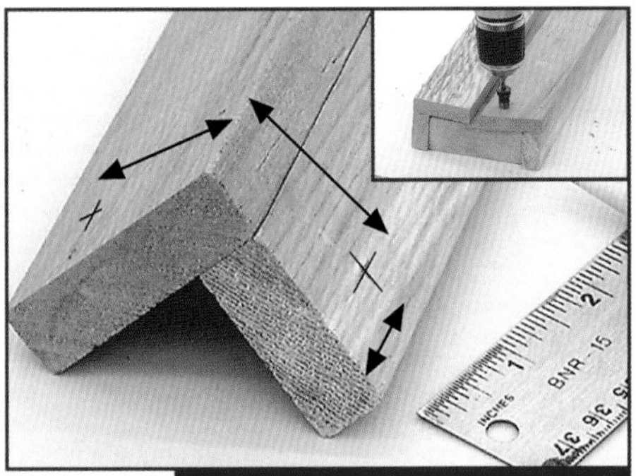

Pre-Drill

Step 10 - On each side of the top leg corner measure 1½" in and ¾" down from the top and mark.

Step 11 - Pre-drill and countersink (T) where marked, as shown in the photo inset. It helps to put a block under the legs when drilling.

Step 12 - Sand the legs through 220-grit sandpaper.

Material List		Wood	Quantity	T x W x L
A	legs	redwood	6	5/8" x 3 3/8" x 48"
B	leg block	redwood	1	1 1/2" x 3 3/4" x 3 3/4"
C	skirt base	redwood	1	3/4" x 5 3/8" x 5 3/8"
D	long skirt	redwood	2	5/8" x 2 1/2" x 6 5/8"
E	short skirt	redwood	2	5/8" x 2 1/2" x 5 3/8"
F	top	redwood	1	3/4" x 5 3/8" x 5 3/8"
G	long bottom brace	redwood	2	5/8" x 1 1/8" x 15 7/8"
H	short bottom brace	redwood	2	5/8" x 1 1/8" x 14 5/8"
I	gazing ball resting block	redwood	1	1 1/2" x 3 1/2" x 3 1/2"
J	middle braces	redwood	2	5/8" x 1 1/8" x 9"
K	leaves*	redwood	6	5/8" x 2 1/2" x 4"
Supply List				
L	copper tubing			3/8" diam. x 12"
M	round steel rods		4	1/8" diam. x 48"
N	stainless steel gazing ball		1	6" diam.
O	copper tube strap		2	3/8"
P	brads			1"
Q	wood screws			1 1/4", 1 5/8", 2"
R	clear silicone adhesive			
S	Forstner bit			1 3/8"
T	countersink bit			
U	brass round head wood screws			1/2"
V	redwood sealer			

* Pattern needed for this project is located in pattern packet.

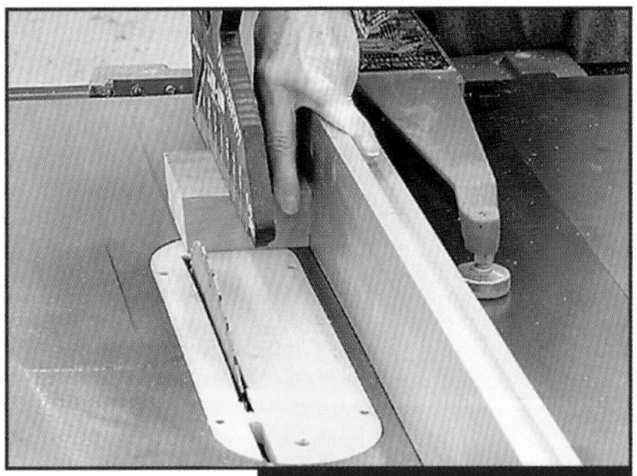

Cut Leg Block

Step 13 - Cut the leg block (B) to the dimensions given in the material list. With the blade set at an 8-degree angle, set the fence on the left side of the table saw. Put the fence 3 3/16" away from the bottom of the blade. Raise the blade high enough to cut through the block. Cut one side, rotate, and cut again until all four sides are mitered.

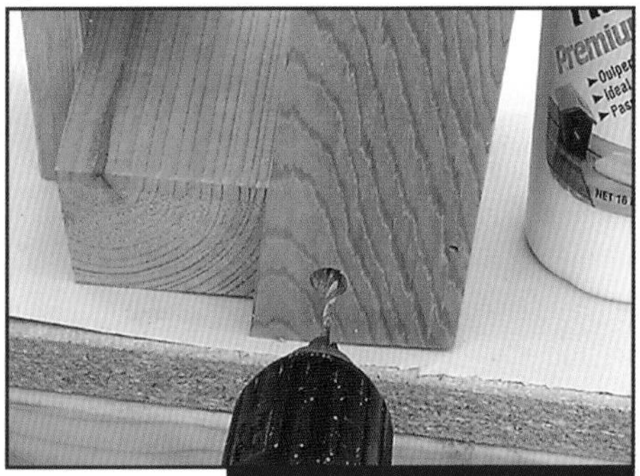

Attach Legs

Step 14 - Set the leg block upside down on a flat surface. Set one leg, in each corner, one at a time. Pre-drill through the countersunk holes.

Step 15 - Glue and screw all four legs in place, using 1⅝" wood screws (Q).

Pre-Drill Skirt Base

Step 16 - Cut the skirt base (C) to the dimensions given in the material list. Center the skirt base on top of the leg block.

Step 17 - Center and measure in 1½" from the two opposing sides. Mark as shown in the photo inset. Pre-drill and countersink where marked.

Attach Skirt Base

Step 18 - Glue and screw the base in place using 1¼" screws (Q).

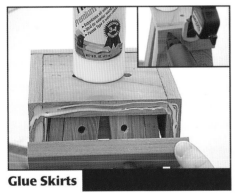

Glue Skirts

Step 19 - Cut the long and short skirt blanks (D, E) to the dimensions given in the material list.

Step 20 - Glue and brad the short skirt pieces in place, and clamp to help hold, as shown in the photo inset.

Side View

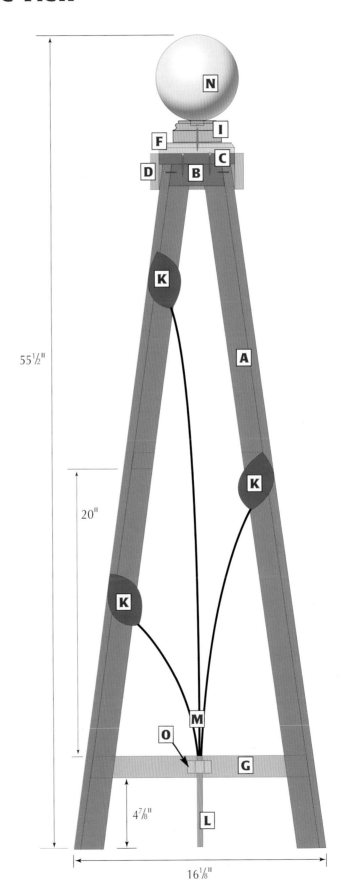

Brad Skirts

Step 21 - Next, glue and brad the long skirt pieces in place, as shown here and in Step 20.

Countersink Top

Step 22 - Cut the top (F) to the dimensions given in the material list. Center and mark 1" from the left and right of center for the screw holes, as shown in the photo inset. Make sure these holes are not on top of the skirt base screws.

Step 23 - Countersink and pre-drill the top.

Rout Top

Step 24 - Place a decorative router bit of your choice in the router and rout around the top edges of the top piece. Sand the top.

Attach Top

Step 25 - Center the top on the skirt base. Glue and screw in place, using the 1¼" screws (Q).

Step 26 - Cut the gazing ball resting block (I) to the dimensions given in the material list. Locate the center of the block and mark.

Drill Resting Block

Step 27 - Using a 1⅜" Forstner bit (S) in the drill press, drill a ⅜"-deep hole for the gazing ball to rest in.

Rout Edges

Step 28 - Using the router with the same decorative bit as before, rout around the top edges of the piece.

Step 29 - Sand the resting block through 220-grit sandpaper.

Step 30 - Center the gazing ball resting block on the top with the wood grains going the same direction and pre-drill into the top through the center of the resting hole.

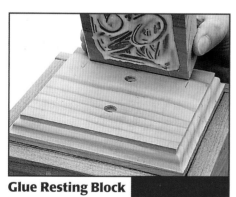

Glue Resting Block

Step 31 - Glue the resting block in place.

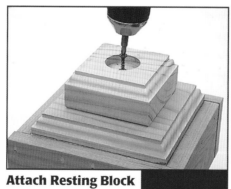

Attach Resting Block

Step 32 - Screw the gazing ball resting block in place using a 2" screw (Q).

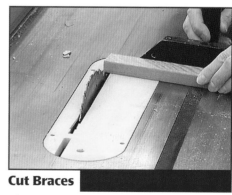

Cut Braces

Step 33 - Cut the long and short bottom braces (G, H) and the middle braces (J) to the dimensions given in the material list. With the miter gauge set at 8 degrees, cut the ends of each brace at an 8-degree angle following the lines of the legs.

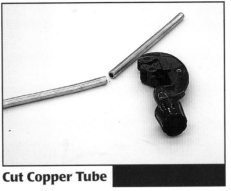

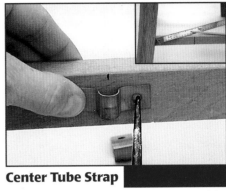

Level Braces

Step 34 - Measure 4⅞" up from the floor surface for brace locations. Level the longer braces. Glue and brad in place.

Step 35 - Glue and brad the short braces in place, lining them up with the long braces, as shown in the photo inset.

Step 36 - Measure up 20" from the top of the lower braces and place the two middle braces on two opposing sides. Brad in place, as with the lower braces.

Cut Copper Tube

Step 37 - Cut two pieces of copper tubing (L) to 6" in length. We used a pipe cutter.

Center Tube Strap

Step 38 - Measure and mark the center of the two long braces, as shown in the photo inset. Center a copper tube strap (O) on the brace and mark for pre-drilling using an awl.

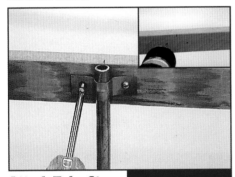

Attach Tube Strap

Step 39 - Pre-drill for the ½" brass wood screws (U) where marked, as shown in the photo inset.

Step 40 - Attach the copper tube strap loosely using the brass screws. Insert the copper tubing and tighten the screws.

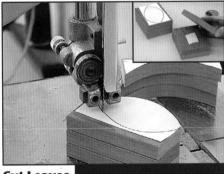

Cut Leaves

Step 41 - Cut the leaf blanks (K) to the dimensions given in the material list. Locate the leaf patterns in the pattern packet and make copies. Gang three blanks together using double-sided tape and adhere the pattern to the ganged blanks using double-sided tape, as shown in the photo inset.

Step 42 - Cut around the leaf pattern using a band saw. Sand the edges to remove any kerf marks.

Drill Leaves

Step 43 - While still ganged together, clamp the leaves to drill for the steel rods. Center and drill a ⅛"-wide by 1½"-deep hole in each leaf base.

Step 44 - Separate the leaves and remove the pattern. Sand the leaves smooth, rounding the edges slightly, through 220-grit sandpaper.

Cut Rods

Step 45 - Using a hack saw, cut the rods (M): two at 36", two at 21", and two at 14" in length.

Insert Rods

Step 46 - Insert the three rods of different lengths into the copper tubing.

Attach Leaves

Step 47 - To attach the leaves, place a drop of glue in the hole at the base of the leaf and insert the rod.

Step 48 - Bending the rods slightly to give some shape to each stem, clamp the leaf to the leg to hold in place while arranging the other stems.

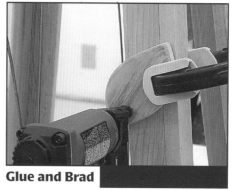

Glue and Brad

Step 49 - Place glue on the part of the leaf that touches the leg and brad the leaf to the leg. Repeat this on the opposite side of the obelisk, creating a mirror image of the first side.

Finish Sealer

Step 50 - Finish as desired using an outdoor sealer. We used a redwood colored stain/sealer (V). Let dry thoroughly.

Gazing Ball

Step 51 - To adhere the stainless steel gazing ball (N) to the obelisk, squeeze out a glob of clear silicone adhesive (R) into the gazing ball rest. Make sure there is enough silicone to attach to the ball itself. Let cure.

Step 52 - Set the obelisk out in your garden and enjoy the wonderful images in the gazing ball.

Window Box

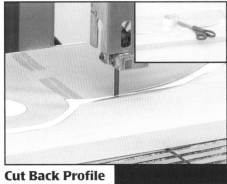

Cut Back Profile

Step 1 - Cut backs (A, B) front (C), and bottom (D) to the dimensions given in the material list.

Step 2 - Locate bottom back pattern in the pattern packet. Adhere the pattern to the bottom back blank using double-sided tape, as shown in the photo inset. Cut along the pattern lines with a band saw.

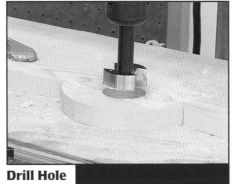

Drill Hole

Step 3 - With the 1⅝" Forstner bit in the drill press, drill the center hole in the bottom back piece.

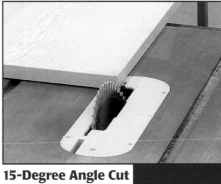

15-Degree Angle Cut

Step 4 - With the table saw blade set at a 15-degree angle, cut the top and the bottom of the front blank. The angles should both go in the same direction.

Box Bottom

Step 5 - With the table saw blade still set at 15 degrees, cut one side of the bottom blank (D) at a 15 degree angle.

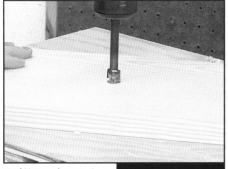

Drill Drain Holes

Step 6 - With the ½" Forstner bit in the drill press, randomly drill six holes in the bottom (D) to allow for drainage. Because of the hanging system, you will need to use a spacer between the house and window box. If your ¾" hanging strip is going on any other trim, allow for that thickness also.

Spacer

Step 7 - Cut the spacer (F) to the dimensions given in the material list. Mark for evenly spaced screws across both sides of the length of the spacer.

Step 8 - Countersink and pre-drill for the screws.

Material List		Wood	Quantity	T x W x L
A	top back	pine	1	¾" x 10¼" x 58"
B	bottom back*	pine	1	¾" x 10¼" x 58"
C	front	pine	1	¾" x 11¼" x 60"
D	bottom	pine	1	¾" x 10" x 56½"
E	sides*	pine	2	¾" x 9½" x 10¼"
F	spacer	redwood	1	¾" x 4" x 58"
G	reinforcement strips	redwood	2	1½" x 1½" x 56½"
H	brackets*	pine	2	1½" x 10" x 11"
I	hanger	redwood	1	¾" x 6" x 58"

Supply List			T x W x L
J	Forstner bit		½", 1⅝"
K	countersink bit		#6
L	galvanized wood screws		#6 x 1⅝", #6 x 2"
M	plug cutter		#6
N	paint (exterior, your color choice)		
O	roofing cement		
P	tar paper		

* Patterns needed for this project are located in pattern packet.

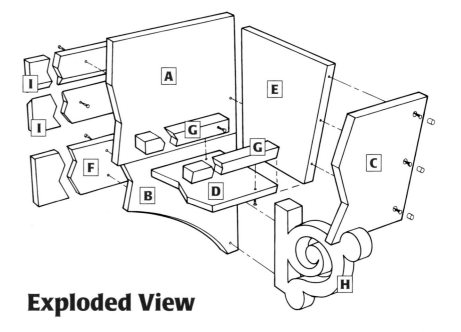

Exploded View

Attach Spacer

Step 9 - Clamp the lower edge of the top back and the upper edge of the bottom back together. Center the spacer over the seam. Glue and screw the spacer to the back pieces.

Countersink

Step 10 - Turn the back over and countersink (deep enough to plug) to the left of the previous screws along the length of both backs. Screw through the front of the backs into the spacer across backs.

Plugs

Step 11 - Using a plug cutter attachment on the drill press, cut plugs, as shown in the photo inset.

Step 12 - After placing glue in the holes, put plug in and tap into place. Let dry and trim plugs flush with back. Sand smooth.

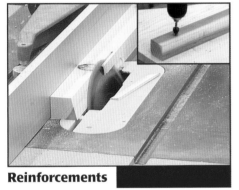

Reinforcements

Step 13 - Cut the two reinforcement strips (G) to the dimensions given in the material list. One of these strips will need to have a 15-degree angle cut along one side.

Step 14 - Countersink evenly spaced holes across one side of the back strip, not the one with the angle, as shown in the photo inset.

Screw Together

Step 15 - Turn the pre-drilled strip once and set the bottom piece on both strips. Line up the angled front of the one strip with the angled bottom piece. The back pieces are also flush.

Step 16 - Countersink and pre-drill from the bottom into the strips. Screw together using galvanized wood screws (L), as shown in the photo inset.

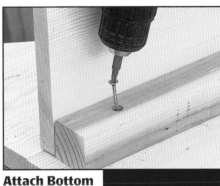

Attach Bottom

Step 17 - Place the back edge of the bottom just over the seam on the back piece. Leave a ¾" space in from each side to allow room for the side pieces. Screw the bottom to the back through the previously countersunk holes (Step 14).

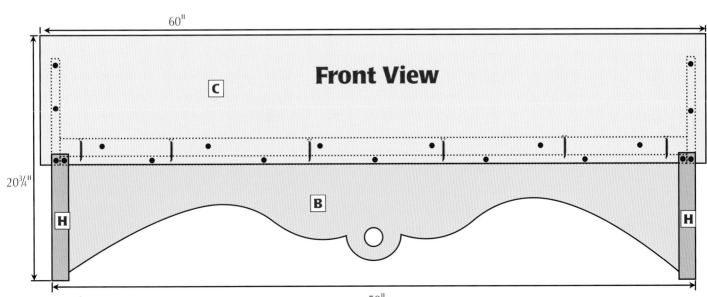

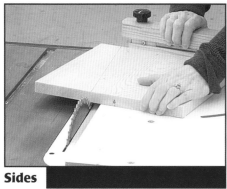

Sides

Step 18 - Cut the sides (E) to the dimensions given in the material list. Use the pattern located in the pattern packet or set up an angle jig to cut a 15-degree angle off one side of the side blanks.

Hanger Bar

Step 24 - Countersink evenly staggered holes along the top hanger. Place hanger on back with the top of the hanger just slightly lower than the top of the back, with the 45-degree angle facing down. Screw hanger to the back.

Step 25 - Cut the brackets (H) to the dimensions on the material list. Locate the bracket pattern in the pattern packet and adhere it to the blanks with double-stick tape.

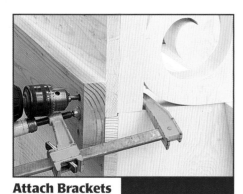

Attach Brackets

Step 27 - Attach the brackets by placing them under the box, flush with the sides, and clamp to hold. Refer to the side view drawing for screw locations and pre-drill through the back into the bracket. We replaced the first screw with a longer one as it goes through the spacer. Sand the window box through 220-grit sandpaper. Finish as desired. Let dry.

Attach Sides

Step 19 - Referring to the side view drawing, mark the screw locations on the sides. Countersink for plugs, as shown in the photo inset.

Step 20 - Set the sides in place and screw sides to the bottom and reinforcement strips.

Step 21 - Fill the sides with plugs as before. Trim and sand smooth.

Step 22 - Center the front on the sides. Countersink and pre-drill evenly spaced holes along the side and front bottom edges. Refer to the front view drawing for placement. Screw the front to the sides and bottom. Fill with plugs and trim. Sand smooth.

Scroll Saw

Step 26 - Drill access holes for the scroll saw blade and, using the scroll saw, cut along the pattern lines. Sand brackets.

Seal Inside

Step 28 - These next two steps are optional. Tape off inside the box around the top and, using roof cement (O) and a putty knife, coat the inside of the box. This will help to keep the wood waterproof.

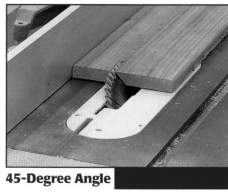

45-Degree Angle

Step 23 - Cut the hanger (I) to the dimensions given in the material list. With the table saw blade set at a 45-degree angle, cut down the center of the hanger, as shown. This will give you the piece that attaches to the window box and the piece to attach to your house.

Side View

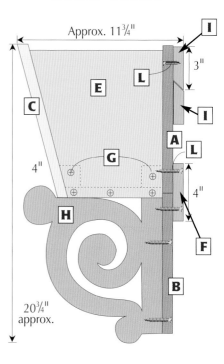

Step 29 - When attaching the hanger piece to the house, place a strip of tar paper (P) between the house and hanger to help keep water damage and dry rot away from the wall of the house.

Redwood Foot Bridge

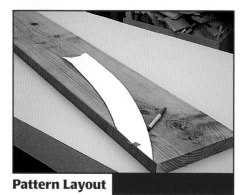

Pattern Layout

Step 1 - Cut the side supports (A) to the dimensions given in the material list. Locate the halved side support in the pattern packet and adhere to the side blank. Trace around the pattern with a marker. Flip the pattern end for end, then line up the centers and trace the other side.

Material List		Wood	Quantity	T x W x L
A	side supports*	redwood	2	1½" x 9¼" x 60"
B	slats	redwood	7	¾" x 7⅜" x 32"
C	cross braces	redwood	7	1½" x 11¹¹/₁₆" x 30½"
D	wood plugs	redwood	14	⅜" diam. x ⅜"
Supply List				
E	wood screws		38	#7 x 2½"
F	wood screws		4	#6 x 1¼"
G	wood glue			

*Pattern needed for this project is located in pattern packet.

Band Sawing

Step 2 - Use the band saw to cut out one side support. Use a drum sander chucked into the drill press to smooth the sawn edges.

Tracing

Step 3 - Use the one cut-out side support as a template to trace the second side support. Use the band saw to cut out the second side support, as shown in Step 2.

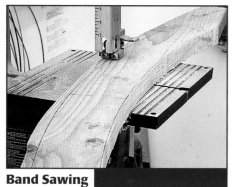

Rabbeting

Step 4 - Use the router to make a ¾"-wide by ¾"-deep rabbet along the inside top edge of both side supports. Make several passes, working the wood down to prevent any tearout.

Step 5 - Cut the redwood slats (B) to the dimensions given in the material list.

Countersinking

Step 6 - Each slat gets two pre-drilled screw holes. Measure in from the end ⅜" and 1½" up and down from the long edge. Use the drill press with a ⅜" countersink bit to predrill. Countersink to allow the screw head to sit flush with the surface.

Assembly

Step 7 - Evenly space the slats on the side supports. Pre-drill and screw the slats to the side supports with the wood screws (E). When you get down to the two end slats, you'll need to use the wood screws (F) on the very last two screw locations. Slightly angle inward during the pre-drilling to make sure the screws do not go through the bottom of the side supports.

Front View

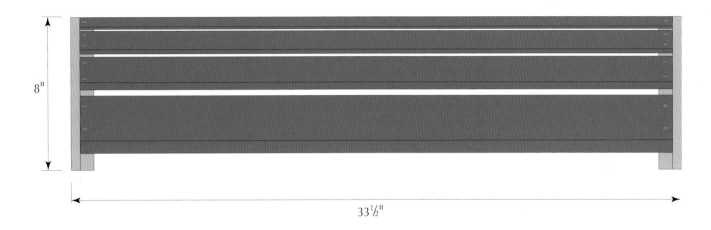

8"

33½"

Side View

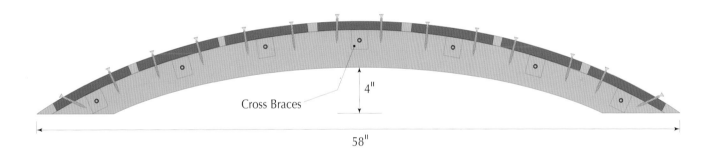

Cross Braces

4"

58"

Support Screws

Step 8 - Cut the cross braces (C) to the dimensions given in the material list. To help support each slat, a brace is screwed to the inside of side supports. Center each brace under each slat and countersink a screw location with a ⅜" countersink bit to a depth of approximately ⅜".

Support Assembly

Step 9 - Use the 2½" wood screws (E) to fasten each slat brace in place.

Wood Plugs

Step 10 - Use the drill press with a ⅜" plug-cutting bit and a scrap piece of redwood to make the 14 wooden plugs (D). Use some glue and a mallet to hammer the plugs in place. We decided to let the bridge naturally weather; however, you can use an exterior finish to protect it from the outdoor elements. (Add reinforcements if the bridge will have to handle human weight.)

Garden Hose Guides

material list

material list	Wood	Quantity	T x W x L
A hose guides	redwood	4	3½" x 3½" x 21¼"
B post caps	redwood	4	3½" x 3½"

Supply List

C	Liquid Nail adhesive
D	transparent stain (heart redwood by Superdeck)

Side view

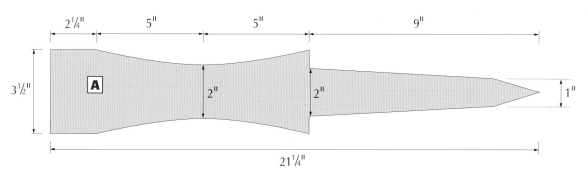

2¼"   5"   5"   9"

3½"   A   2"   2"   1"

21¼"

Cross Cutting

Step 1 - The hose guides are made out of 4 x 4 redwood blanks. Cut the hose guides (A) to the dimensions given in the material list. Use the radial arm saw with a stop block to make the four cuts.

Centers

Step 2 - Locate the centers on both ends of each hose guide by drawing diagonally from corner to corner.

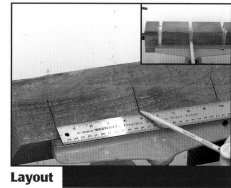

Layout

Step 3 - Refer to the drawing above for the different layout points on the hose guides. Use a pencil to make marks. Use the mitered gouge to bring the wood down to the proper depth on the marks, as shown in the inset photo.

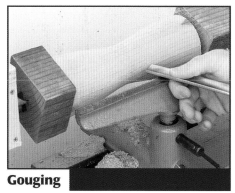

Gouging

Step 4 - Use a gouge to rough out the profile on the hose guide portion.

Stake Profile

Step 5 - Use the round gouge to make the profile. Refer to the side view drawing for diameters.

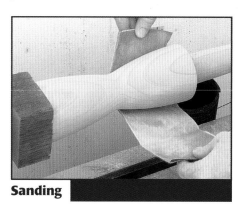

Sanding

Step 6 - Sand the surface smooth while the piece is still attached to the lathe. Apply a protective finish. Use liquid nail to adhere post caps to hose guides after they are placed in ground.

Potting Bench

Mark Half-Laps

Step 1 - Cut the back bench support (A), upper and lower back rails (B, C), and back stiles (D) to the dimensions given in the material list.

Step 2 - A series of middle or T half-laps are used to join the stiles to the upper and lower back rails and the back bench support. Laying out the pieces on the floor will make the marking job easier. Refer to the drawing and the piece drawings in the pattern packet for the half-lap locations and mark for placements. The rabbet on the end of each stile is made on the front of the boards. The mating dado is cut into the back of the upper rail and bottom shelf support.

Material List		Quantity	T x W x L
A	back bench support*		1½" x 5½" x 40"
B	upper back rail*		1½" x 3½" x 40"
C	lower back rail*		1½" x 3½" x 33⅜"
D	back stiles *	2	1½" x 3½" x 44¾"
E	bottom shelf support		1½" x 3½" x 40"
F	back legs	2	1½" x 5½" x 72"
G	bench cleats	2	1½" x 5½" x 4"
H	bench side skirts	2	1½" x 5½" x 21½"
I	front legs	2	1½" x 5½" x 32½"
J	bottom side shelf supports	2	1½" x 3½" x 19¾"
K	bottom shelf boards	6	1½" x 3½" x 40"
L	bench front skirt		1½" x 5½" x 46"
M	bench back surface board	1	1½" x 3½" x 40"
N	bench surface boards	5	1½" x 3½" x 47½"
O	top shelf boards	2	1½" x 5½" x 47½"
P	top shelf board		1½" x 3½" x 47½"
Supply List			
Q	hanging plant brackets	2	17"
R	exterior deck screws		6 x 1¼", 6 x 2"
S	trellis (cut down to 60")		19½" x 72"
T	copper tube strap	6	¼"
U	deck stain or sealer		

* Drawings needed for this project are located in pattern packet.

Upper Back Rail

Step 3 - Using a ¾" dado blade and a sliding miter table on the table saw, set the blade to a height of ¾".

Step 4 - Run the upper back rail (B) through the dado blade, being careful to line up the blade with your marks. Repeat for other end of rail.

Step 5 - Cut the matching rabbet on the upper end of the back stiles (D), as shown in the photo inset.

Lower Stile Half-Lap

Step 6 - Cut the back stile lower rabbet. Repeat for other back stile. Cut the matching dadoes in the back bench support (A).

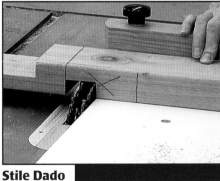

Stile Dado

Step 7 - Cut the middle dadoes in the back stiles.

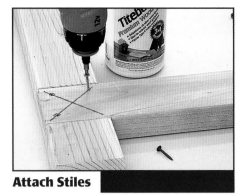

Attach Stiles

Step 8 - Cut the matching rabbets on both ends of the lower back rail (C).

Step 9 - Glue the back stiles to the upper back rail with wood glue and refer to the back view drawing for the screw locations. An easy way to mark for screws is to draw an X from corner to corner and measure in ¾" from the sides. Pre-drill and attach the stile to the rail using 1¼" screws (R).

Glue and Screw

Step 10 - Glue the stiles to the back bench support. Mark for screws, as shown in Step 9. Pre-drill and attach stile to rail using 1¼" screws (R).

Lower Back Rail

Step 11 - Repeating the previous step, attach the lower back rail to the stiles.

Step 12 - Sand this center section through 220-grit sandpaper.

Layout and Mark

Step 13 - Cut the bottom shelf support (E) and the back legs (F) to the dimensions given in the material list.

Step 14 - Lay pieces out on the floor. Line up the center section with the top of the back legs and bottom shelf support 6½" up from the bottom of the back legs.

Attach Back Legs

Step 15 - Mark for screw placements. Attach the center section to the back legs using wood glue and 2" screws (R). Attach the bottom shelf support to the legs, as shown in the photo inset.

Back View

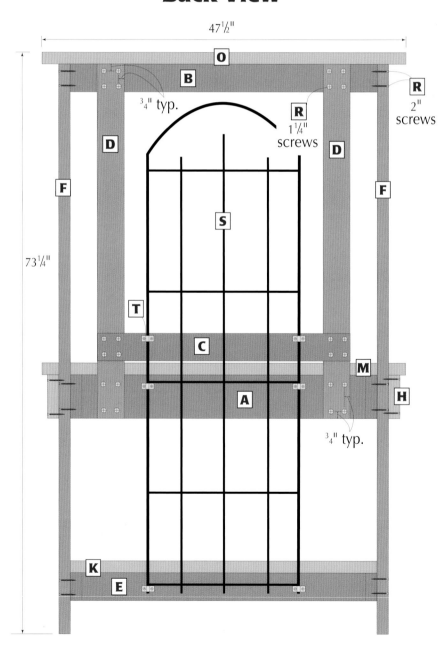

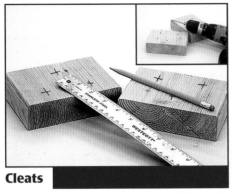

Cleats

Step 16 - Cut the bench cleats (G) to the dimensions given in the material list. Sand. Mark for three screws so that they do not interfere with screws used later. Refer to the exploded drawing for placements. Pre-drill cleats.

Attach Bench Cleats

Step 17 - Set the bench cleats on the back bench support against each of the legs. Attach the bench cleats to the back leg using wood glue and 2" wood screws.

Attach Side Skirt

Step 18 - Cut the bench side skirts (H) to the dimensions given in the material list. Refer to the side view drawing for screw placement. Mark for screw placement, as shown in the photo inset.

Step 19 - Clamp side skirts in place. Pre-drill through side skirts into back legs.

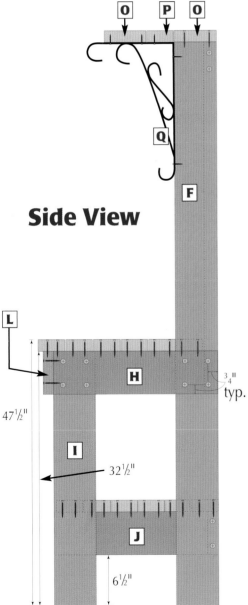

Side View

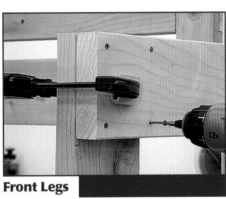

Front Legs

Step 20 - Cut the front legs (I) to the dimensions given in the material list. Clamp the front legs to the side skirts and attach by gluing, pre-drilling, and screwing through the skirts into the legs with 2" screws.

Bottom Side Supports

Step 21 - Cut the bottom side shelf supports (J) to the dimensions given in the material list. Mark for screw placement. Clamp the bottom side shelf support to the inside of the legs. Level, then glue and screw in place.

Bottom Shelf

Step 22 - Cut the bottom shelf boards (K) to the dimensions given in the material list. Starting at the back, place the shelf boards over the bottom shelf support. Use a nail between the boards as a spacer. Pre-drill and screw in place.

Attach Front Skirt

Step 23 - Cut the bench front skirt (L) to the dimensions given in the material list. Attach the front skirt to the side skirts by marking for screws, pre-drilling, gluing, and screwing in place. Clamp until dry.

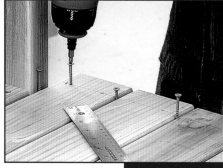

Attach Bench Top

Step 24 - Cut the bench surface boards (M,N) to the dimensions given in the material list. Place the shorter board between the back legs, flush with the back bench support. Using screws as spacers, place the other surface boards with a ¾" overhang on the sides and front. Refer to the exploded drawing for screw placements; mark, pre-drill and screw the boards in place.

Hanging Shelf Bracket

Step 25 - Attach the hanging brackets (Q) to the front of the back legs. Making sure brackets are level with the top of the legs, pre-drill and screw the brackets in place, using 1¼" screws (R). (You might have to drill holes in your brackets depending on which brackets you buy.)

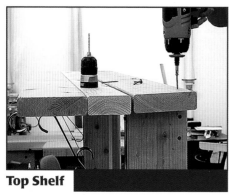

Top Shelf

Step 26 - Cut the top shelf boards (O, P) to the dimensions given in the material list. Place a 5½" board over the top of the legs, flush with the upper back rail and a 1¾" overhang on the sides. Using screws as spacers

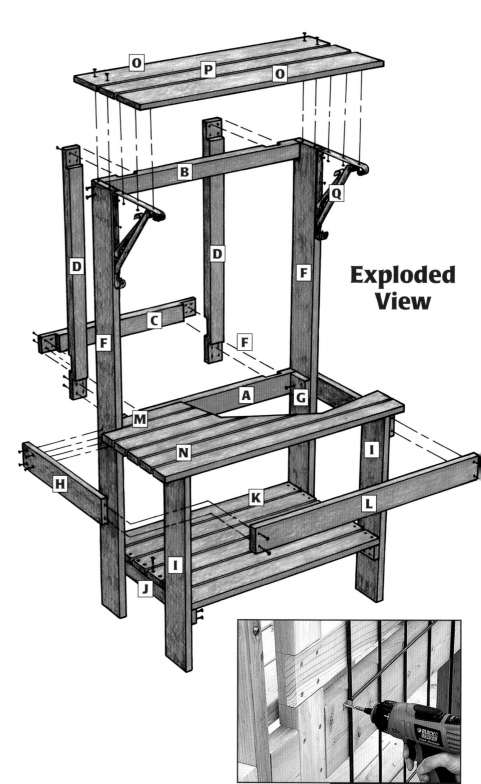

Exploded View

again, put the 3½" board in place, followed by the other 5½" board. Pre-drill and screw the boards in place. Check the exploded drawing for screw direction.

Attach Trellis

Step 27 - Using a hack saw, we cut 12" from the bottom legs and one butterfly off our trellis to make it fit. Center the trellis (S) on the back between the back stiles and clamp in place. Using copper tube straps (T), pre-drill and screw trellis in place.

Step 28 - Sand the potting bench, rounding the edges. Finish with your choice of deck stain or sealer.

This Bath is for the Birds

Cut Post

Step 1 - Using a radial arm saw, cut the post (A) to the length given in the material list.

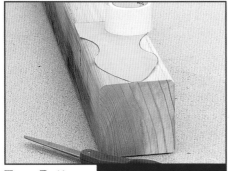

Tape Pattern

Step 2 - Locate the post pattern in the pattern packet and adhere it to the bottom of the post with double-sided tape.

Note: This article shows two methods of transferring patterns to your wood blanks. You might also want to just copy our pattern four times and adhere the copies to the blanks with double-sided tape.

Band Saw

Step 3 - Using a band saw, cut each side of the post along the pattern, ending at the bottom of the post. A couple of roller supports were needed to help hold the post behind the saw.

Material List	Wood	Quantity	T x W x L
A post*	redwood	1	3¹⁄₂" x 3¹⁄₂" x 44"
B legs*	redwood	4	1¹⁄₂" x 11" x 13"
C arms*	redwood	4	1¹⁄₂" x 7³⁄₈" x 8"

Supply List			
D wood screws		16	#8 x 2"
E 16" round glazed tray		1	
F cardboard or transfer paper			
G countersink bit			³⁄₈"
H Superdeck® exterior transparent stain (red cedar)			

* Patterns needed for this project are located in pattern packet.

Side view

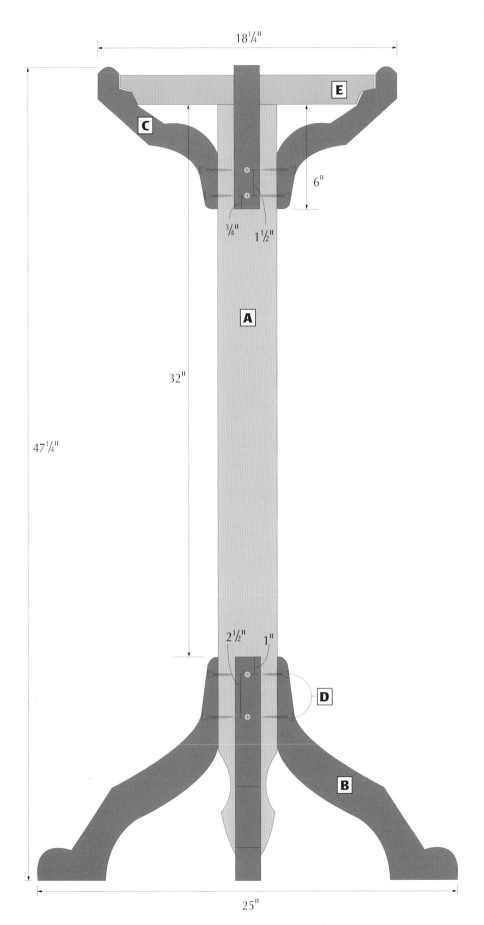

18¼"

E

C

6"

¾" 1½"

A

32"

47¼"

2½" 1"

D

B

25"

Tape Cut-Offs

Step 4 - When you are finished cutting both sides of the pattern, carefully remove the pattern and tape the cut-offs back onto the post using masking tape. This will give you a solid form to continue your cutting.

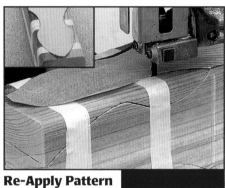

Re-Apply Pattern

Step 5 - Turn the post on its side and re-apply the pattern, as shown in the photo inset.

Step 6 - Cut along the pattern lines again, using the band saw.

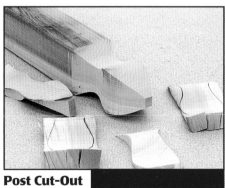

Post Cut-Out

Step 7 - Remove the tape and pattern and you have your decorative post.

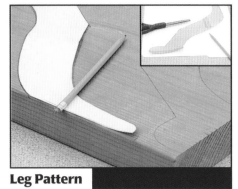

Leg Pattern

Step 8 - Cut leg blank (B) to the dimensions given in the material list.

Step 9 - Locate the leg pattern in the pattern packet. Trace the leg pattern onto a piece of cardboard, as shown in the photo inset. Cut out the cardboard pattern.

Step 10 - Place the pattern on the leg blank and trace four times.

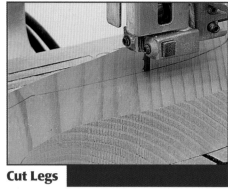

Cut Legs

Step 11 - Cut the leg profiles using a band saw.

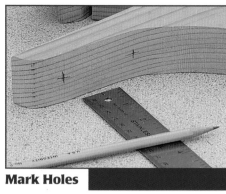

Mark Holes

Step 12 - Mark the screw placements. Refer to the side view drawing for screw locations.

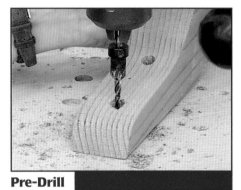

Pre-Drill

Step 13 - Using a ⅜" countersink bit in the drill press, pre-drill through all four legs.

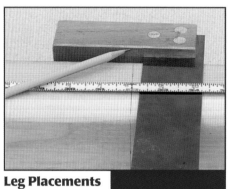

Leg Placements

Step 14 - Measure down 32" from the top of the post and mark for leg placements.

Step 15 - This is a good time to sand the legs and post through 220-grit sandpaper.

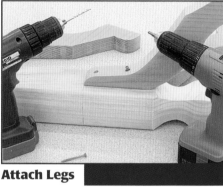

Attach Legs

Step 16 - Align the legs with the marks and pre-drill using a ⅛" bit.

Step 17 - Screw the legs to the post with wood screws (D).

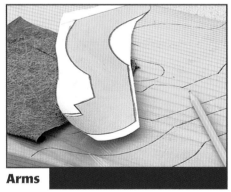

Arms

Step 18 - Cut arm blanks (C) to the dimensions given in the material list.

Step 19 - Locate the arm pattern in the pattern packet. Double check to make sure this pattern works with your tray. There may be slight differences. Adjust the pattern accordingly.

Step 20 - Transfer the pattern to the blank, four times, using transfer paper.

Pre-Drill

Step 21 - Mark the screw placements, referring to the side view drawing for the screw locations.

Step 22 - Using the same countersink bit (G) that was used for the legs, pre-drill through the arms. Sand arms through 220-grit sandpaper.

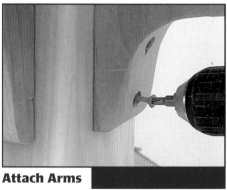

Attach Arms

Step 23 - Measure down 6" from the top of post and mark the arm placement.

Step 24 - Pre-drill and screw the arms on the post with wood screws (D).

Step 25 - Finish with a deck stain and sealer. Let dry. Set tray (E) in arms and fill with water. The tray can also hold birdseed instead of water.

Squirrel Feeder

Sides

Step 1 - Cut the sides (A), bottom (B), back (C), bench (D), lid (E), stretcher (F), and the plexiglass (G) to the dimensions given in the material list. The sides have three dadoes to hold the bottom, back, and plexiglass in place. Two ⅜" dadoes will receive the rabbets on the bottom blank and the back blank. Cut the ⅜" x ⅜" deep dadoes in the sides with the table saw, adjusting the fence to make the dadoes ⅜" from the edge of the bottom side and the back side of both inside blanks. The dadoes that receive the plexiglass are cut by using the table saw with a ⅛" kerf size blade. Cut the ⅛" x ⅜" deep dadoes ⅜" in from the front inside edge of both side blanks.

Bottom

Step 2 - The bottom blank rabbets are cut using the router table and a ⅜" rabbeting router bit. Make the first rabbet along the underside of the back edge ⅜" x ⅜" deep; this rabbet is to receive a dado in the back blank. The two side rabbets on the underside are cut the same as the back edge, except you'll make a stopped rabbet. Cut the ⅜" x ⅜" deep rabbets starting on the back edge, working your way toward the front to a length of 7". Do the same for the other side. Refer to exploded drawing.

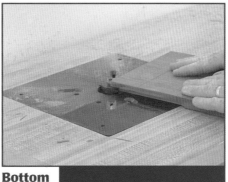

Back

Step 3 - The back blank receives a through ⅜" x ⅜" deep dado along the inside bottom. Make this cut using the table saw and adjust the fence so that the dado is ⅜" up from the bottom inside blank. The back blank also receives two rabbets in the inside of both sides so it can slide into the dadoes of the side blanks (A). Cut the two ⅜" x ⅜" deep rabbets using the router table and a ⅜" router bit. Make the rabbets on the outside edges of the back, referring to Step 4 for reference.

30-Degree Miter

Step 4 - The back blank also receives a miter cut along the top edge. Measure up from the bottom 6" to allow clearance for the lid to open properly. To make the cut, use the table saw with the blade tilted to 30 degrees, with the miter fence set to 90 degrees. Refer to the side view drawing. Drill two ¼" holes through the back of the back blank, 1" down from the top edge, centered, with a 2" space between them; this will allow you to use screws to mount the piece.

Material List	**Quantity**	**T x W x L**
Wood:		
A sides	2	¾"x 6"x 6½"
B bottom	1	¾"x 7³⁄₁₆"x 14¼"
C back	1	¾"x 7¼"x 6½"
D bench	1	¾"x 5¼"x 7³⁄₁₆"
E lid	1	¾"x 6⅞"x 9"
F stretcher	1	¾"x 1½"x 6½"
G plexiglass	1	⅛"x 3¼"x 7¼"
Supply List		
H hinge	1	3"
I dowel	1	¼" diam. x 6"
J dowel	1	⅜" diam. x 10"

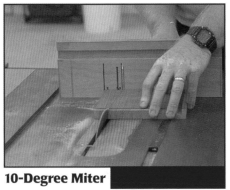

10-Degree Miter

Step 5 - Both side blanks (A) are mitered 10 degrees along the top so the lid will rest at a slight angle to allow rainwater runoff. Using double-stick carpet tape, transfer the pattern from the pattern packet plans to the blanks. Make several copies of the side blank plans in case one should tear. Cut the miter using the table saw and miter fence; adjust the miter fence so that it aligns with the lines on the pattern packet plans. Cut along the line, staying just to the outside. Sand flush to the line.

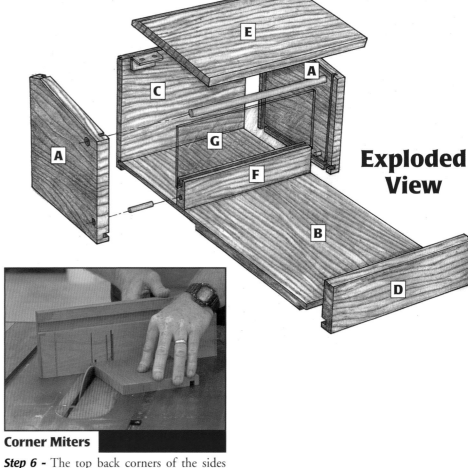

Exploded View

Corner Miters

Step 6 - The top back corners of the sides must be mitered at 30 degrees to allow the proper clearance for the lid to open. Make the cut using the table saw and miter fence. With the fence set to 60 degrees, make the cut just to the outside the line. Sand flush to the line.

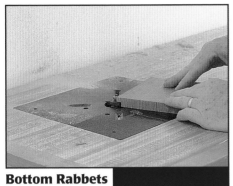

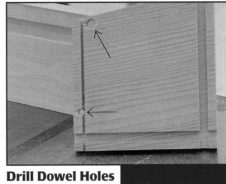

Bottom Rabbets

Step 7 - The bottom (B) receives a rabbet on the underside front edge. This is to receive the dado from the bench. Cut the ⅜" x ⅜" deep rabbet using the router table and a ⅜" router bit. Make a through rabbet. Refer to the exploded drawing.

Bench Dado

Step 8 - The bench is where the squirrel will sit while eating his favorite treat. To make the dado in the bench, use a larger piece of blank for safety. Using the table saw, make a ⅜" x ⅜" deep through dado. Adjust the fence so it will allow the dado to start ⅜" up from the bottom edge. Cut to final dimensions of ¾" x 2¼" x 7³⁄₁₆".

Drill Dowel Holes

Step 9 - The two drill holes in each side receive dowels that help support the feeder and protect the squirrel from the plexiglass. Use the drill press to drill the ⅜" and ¼" holes. The ¼" holes are measured up from the bottom edge 1½" and in from the front edge ⅜". These holes will support the two ¼" x 1¼" long dowels. The ¼" dowels are to be inserted into the stretcher that sits on top of the bottom blank and between the two side blanks. Refer to the exploded drawing. The ⅜" dowel hole, measured in from the front edge ¾" and down from the top edge ¼" centered, runs across the top to protect the squirrel from coming in contact with the plexiglass.

Lid Miter

Step 10 - The lid receives a 30-degree miter cut along its top edge to allow proper clearance for it to open. Make the cut so that the miter starts at the top edge as shown above. The cut is made using the table saw with the blade tilted to 30 degrees. Refer to the exploded drawing.

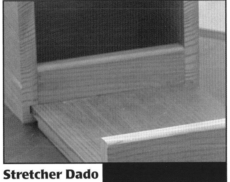

Stretcher Dado

Step 11 - The stretcher receives a through ¼" x ⅜" deep dado along its top edge, centered, to house the bottom edge of the plexiglass. Make the dado using the table saw and a ¼" kerf size blade, adjusting the fence to allow the dado to be centered along the top edge. Dry-fit the stretcher between the two side blanks and use an awl through the two ¼" holes on the sides to locate the corresponding holes in the stretcher. Remove the stretcher and drill the ¼" x ½" deep holes using the drill press.

Hinge Assembly

Step 12 - The hinge gets attached to the back top edge and to the lid's back edge. Be sure to center-punch the holes and pre-drill. The part of the hinge that attaches to the back blank needs to be raised up from flush ³⁄₁₆" to allow for the hinge assembly to work properly. Test fit the assembly, then glue all dadoes and dowels except those dadoes that receive the plexiglass. Clamp the assembly and allow to dry. Attach the hinge and slide in the plexiglass. Sand the entire piece, rounding over any sharp edges, weatherproof the exterior, mount it to a nearby fence or tree, fill the squirrel feeder with some treats, sit back and enjoy watching your new furry friends.

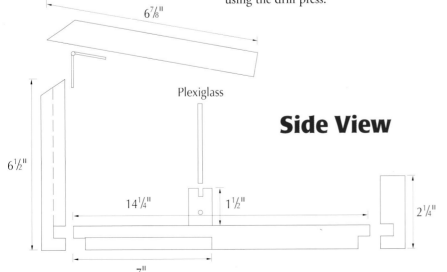

Side View

6⅞"

Plexiglass

6½"

14¼"

1½"

2¼"

7"

The Garden's Delight Butterfly House

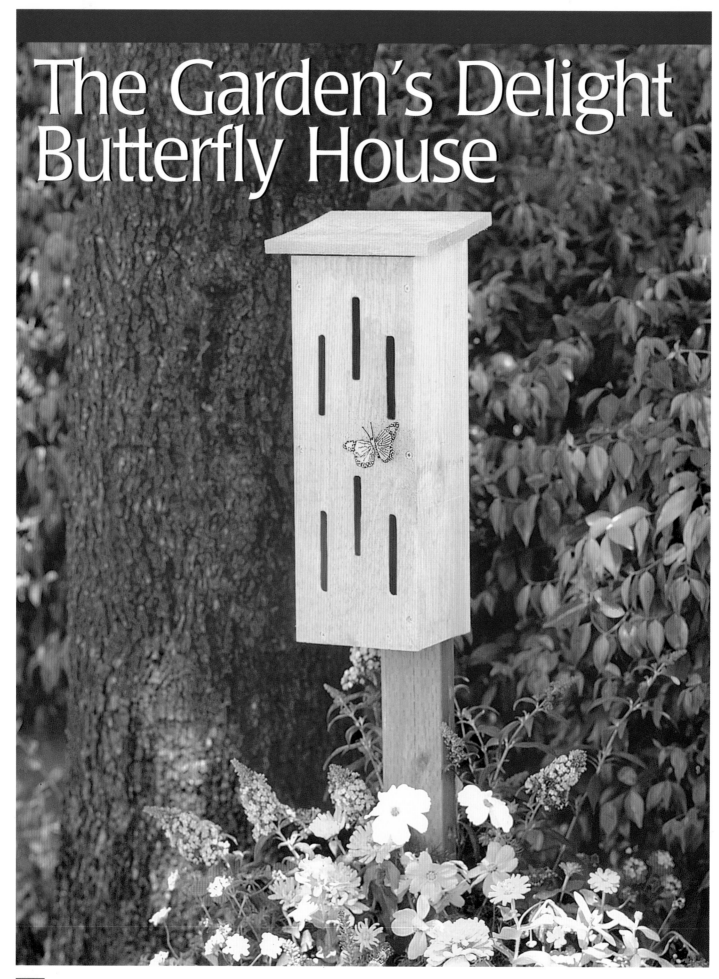

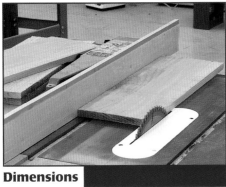

Dimensions

Step 1 - Cut the front (A), sides (B), and back (C), to the dimensions given in the material list. Use the radial arm saw to cut the lengths and a table saw to cut the widths. (The lengths in the material list on the front, sides, and back are slightly longer than final lengths.)

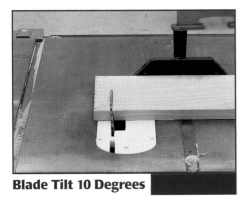

Blade Tilt 10 Degrees

Step 2 - Tilt the table saw blade to 10 degrees. Measure and mark the final length of $18\frac{13}{16}$" to the front blank. Run the top edge of the front blank through the blade. Measure and mark the back blank to the length of 20" and run its top edge through the blade.

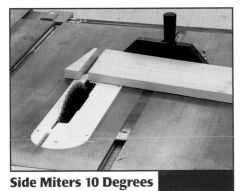

Side Miters 10 Degrees

Step 3 - The sides receive angles to allow the lid to have the proper pitch. Bring the table saw blade back to 90 degrees. Adjust the miter gauge to 10 degrees. Measure and mark the final length of the side blanks to $19\frac{7}{8}$". Run the top edge of each side through the blade.

Material List		Wood	Quantity	T x W x L
Body				
A	front*	redwood	1	$\frac{3}{4}$" x 7" x 21"
B	sides	redwood	2	$\frac{3}{4}$" x 6" x 21"
C	back	redwood	1	$\frac{3}{4}$" x 7" x 21"
D	bottom	redwood	1	$\frac{3}{4}$" x $5\frac{1}{2}$" x 6"
E	lid	redwood	1	$\frac{3}{4}$" x 7" x 9"
F	stake	redwood pressure treated	1	$1\frac{1}{2}$" x $3\frac{1}{2}$" x $40\frac{1}{4}$"
G	small feet	redwood pressure treated	2	$1\frac{1}{2}$" x $3\frac{1}{2}$" x $5\frac{1}{2}$"
H	large feet	redwood pressure treated	2	$1\frac{1}{2}$" x $3\frac{1}{2}$" x 7"
Supply List				
K	hinges		2	1"
L	brass wood screws		16	#8 x $1\frac{1}{4}$"
M	wood screws		16	#6 x $2\frac{1}{2}$"
N	double-sided tape			

* Pattern needed for this project is located in pattern packet.

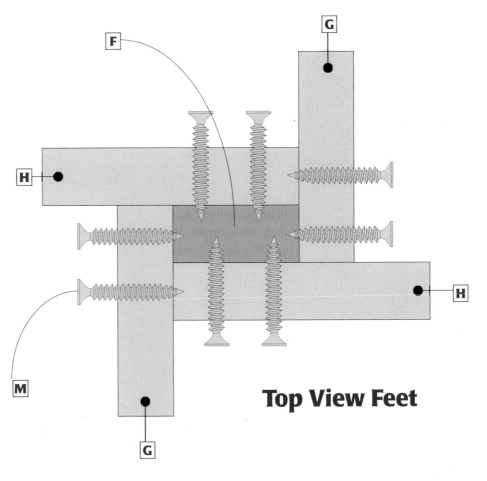

Top View Feet

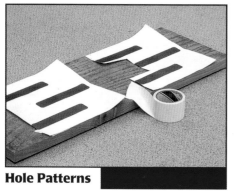

Hole Patterns

Step 4 - Locate the pattern depicting the hole locations for the front blank in the pattern packet and adhere to the front surface of the front blank. Evenly space the two sets of three hole patterns. Use double-sided carpet tape to hold the pattern in place.

Scroll Sawing

Step 5 - Drill inlet holes into each shaded area on the pattern packet. Make sure you use a bit large enough for the saw blade to fit through. Feed the scroll saw blade through the holes and scroll out each shaded area.

Counter Boring

Step 6 - The front and back blanks are fastened to the sides and bottom blanks with the brass screws (L). Refer to the front view house drawing for screw locations. Countersink each hole with a #6 countersinking bit.

Side View House

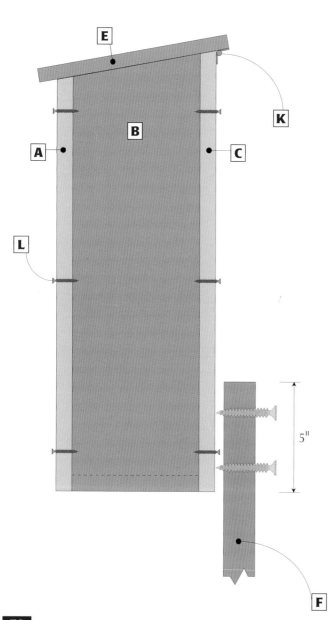

Top View House

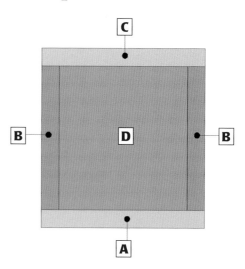

Side View Stake/ Feet Diagram

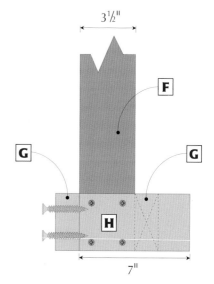

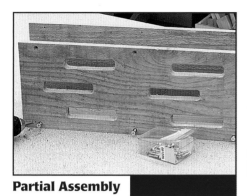

Partial Assembly

Step 7 - Cut the bottom (D) to the dimensions given in the material list. Orient each piece by first laying a side blank down on the worktable. Place the bottom onto the side blank and flush with the side bottom edge; align the front and back blanks flush with the bottom. Screw the brass screws into the sides and bottom.

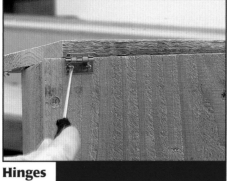

Hinges

Step 8 - Hinges (K) are used on the lid to help in placing the proper feed inside the butterfly house. Cut the lid (E) to the dimensions given in the material list. Each hinge is attached to the back and the lid. Measure in 1" from the back edge for hinge placement. Center the lid on the house and mark for hinge placement.

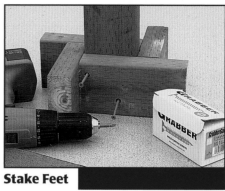

Stake Feet

Step 9 - Cut the stake (F), small stake feet (G), and large stake feet (H) to the dimensions given in the material list. The feet are attached to the bottom of the stake with the wood screws (M).

Front View House

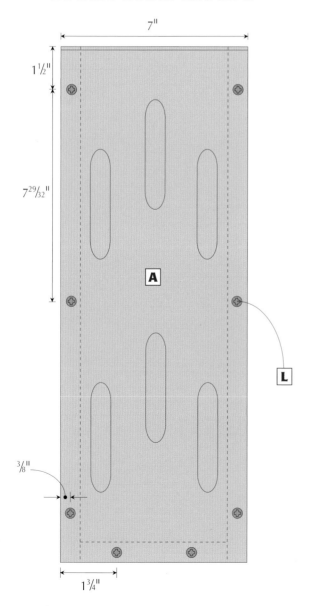

7"

$1\frac{1}{2}$"

$7\frac{29}{32}$"

A

L

$\frac{3}{8}$"

$1\frac{3}{4}$"

Stake Attachment

Step 10 - The opposite end of the stake is attached to the butterfly house with the wood screws (M). Measure up 5" from the bottom of the house. Center the stake on the back blank of the house and fasten it with screws.

All the plants shown in the photo with the finished project are used to attract butterflies. We placed them in a half-barrel purchased at a garden shop. Ask your local garden retail store for the correct plants in your area. Milkweed is what caterpillars eat, which should be planted near the house. A fairly long piece of bark should also be placed inside the house for the cocoon.

Bird House

Cut Material

Step 1 - From a piece of ¾" by 10" by 48" redwood, cut the right top (A), left top (B), front (C), and back (D) to the dimensions given in the material list. Use the table saw to make the ripped and cross cuts.

Cut Perch

Step 2 - Cut the perch (E) out of some ¾" dowel stock to the length given in the material list.

Inlet Hole Location

Step 3 - The front piece has a 2"-diameter hole drilled into it that is located a little off-center. Refer to the front view drawing for the hole location. Transfer the location to the blank. To find the vertical center, draw a line from corner to corner. (Depending on the size of your can, these dimensions can change.)

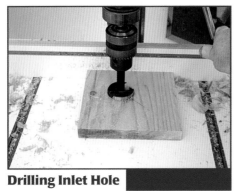

Drilling Inlet Hole

Step 4 - Use the drill press and a 2" Forstner bit to drill the hole in the front.

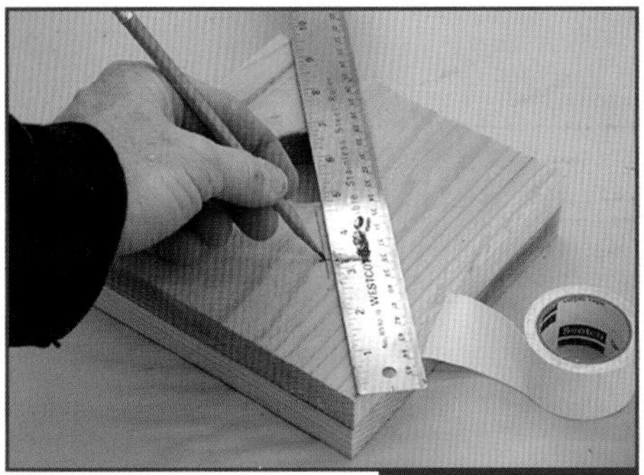

Material List	Wood	Quantity	T x W x L
A right top	redwood		¾" x 8¾" x 10½"
B left top	redwood		¾" x 8" x 10½"
C front	redwood		¾" x 7" x 7"
D back	redwood		¾" x 7" x 7"
E perch			¾" x 12"
Supply List			
F coffee can 1 lb.			5⅛"-O.D. x 6½"
G double-sided tape			
H wood screws		12	#6 x 1⅝"
I wooden plugs		12	⅜" x ¼"
J screw eyes		2	1⅜"
K clothes hanging wire			
L tiles - Delphi Glass			7973B
M Liquid Nail adhesive - Delphi Glass			LN275
N grout and grout sealer - Delphi Glass			425583
O Superdeck exterior semi-transparent stain			coastal gray
P wood glue			
Q Rustoleum spray paint			redwood

Perch Hole Location

Step 5 - Refer to the front view drawing for the perch location. Transfer this location to the front. Gang the front and back pieces together using double-sided tape (G).

Drilling Perch Hole

Step 6 - Use the drill press and a ¹³⁄₁₆" Forstner bit to drill completely through the front piece and ⅜" into the back piece.

Roof Screw Locations

Step 7 - Separate the front and back pieces. Wood screws (H) are used to hold the two roof pieces together and to connect the roof to the front and back. Pre-drill and countersink four screw locations along the edge where the right roof overlaps the left roof. Countersink enough to allow a redwood plug to be inserted to cover the screw head, as shown in the photo inset.

Front and Back Screw Locations

Step 8 - Refer to the side and front view drawings for screw locations that connect the roof to the front and back. Transfer the locations to each roof piece. Pre-drill and countersink these locations. Repeat Step 7 to make the countersinks.

Fastening Roof Pieces

Step 9 - Clamp the two roof pieces together with the right top overhanging the left top. Use the wood screws to fasten the two together.

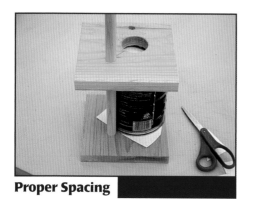

Proper Spacing

Step 10 - Assemble the front, back, and perch pieces together with the coffee can (F) between them. Place a piece of paper between the coffee can and the front and back pieces to allow for expansion.

Shim Up Front and Back

Step 11 - Use a piece of 1" scrap to raise the front and back centered with the roof.

Front View

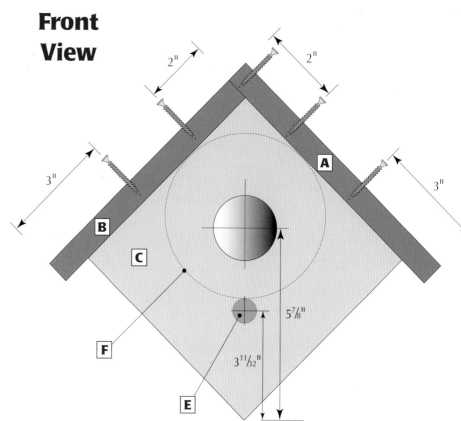

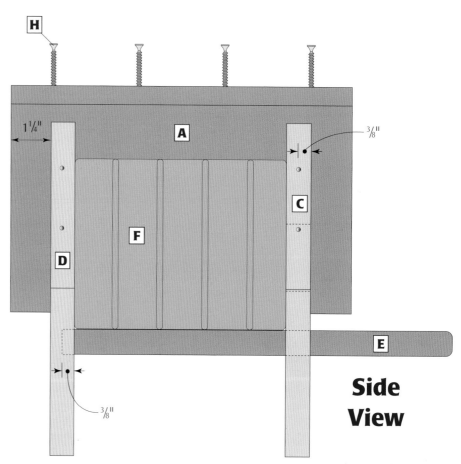

Side View

Fasten Front and Back

Step 12 - Fasten the roof to the front and back with the wood screws.

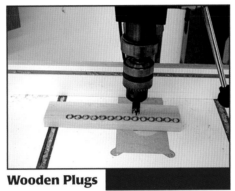

Wooden Plugs

Step 13 - Use the drill press with a ⅜" plug cutting bit and a piece of the off-cut redwood to make the 12 plugs (I).

Fastening Plugs

Step 14 - Use some wood glue (P) and a hammer to insert the plugs over the screw heads.

Step 15 - Sand the plugs flush with the roof and any pencil marks.

Painting Can and Perch

Step 16 - Sand the perch so that it moves very freely in the two holes of the front and back. The more room you can give, the easier it will be to remove the dowel with expansion and shrinkage of the wood.

Step 17 - We chose to paint our coffee can and perch to match more of the environment. Since the perch is not redwood, it may also be a good idea to apply some type of protection from the elements.

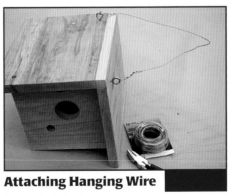

Attaching Hanging Wire

Step 18 - Use the two screw eyes (J) and the clothes wire (K) to hang the bird house from a limb in your tree. Place the screw eyes a fair distance apart and on separate roof tops.

Decorating Coffee Can

Step 19 - As an option, we chose to tile a mosaic pattern around one can using the small tiles (L), Liquid Nail adhesive (M), and grout (N), and also stained the bird house with exterior stain (O). If you do decide to mosaic the coffee can, you will have to move the perch down to allow room for the tiles.

See Pattern Page 1 in Pattern Packet for full-size patterns.

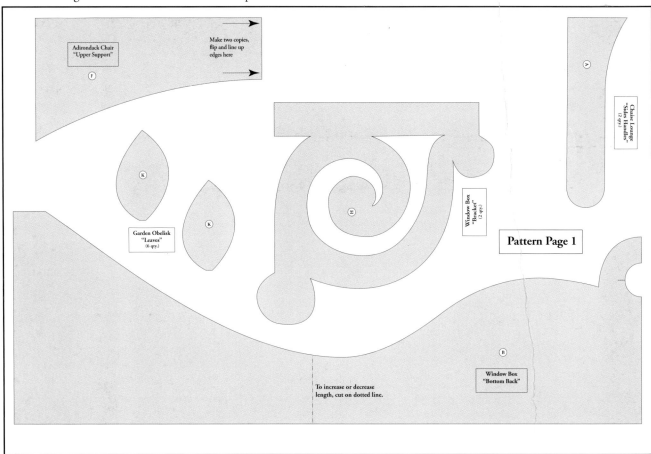

Adirondack Chair
"Upper Support"
F

Make two copies,
flip and line up
edges here

A

Chaise Lounge
"Sides Handles"
(2 qty.)

K

Garden Obelisk
"Leaves"
(6 qty.)

K

H

Window Box
"Bracket"
(2 qty.)

Pattern Page 1

B

Window Box
"Bottom Back"

To increase or decrease
length, cut on dotted line.

See Pattern Page 2 in Pattern Packet for full-size patterns.

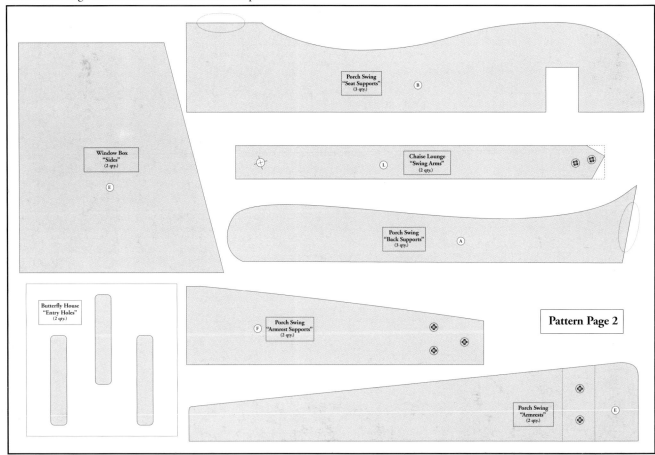

Porch Swing
"Seat Supports"
(3 qty.)
B

Window Box
"Sides"
(2 qty.)
E

L

Chaise Lounge
"Swing Arms"
(2 qty.)

Porch Swing
"Back Supports"
(3 qty.)
A

Butterfly House
"Entry Holes"
(2 qty.)

F

Porch Swing
"Armrest Supports"
(2 qty.)

Pattern Page 2

Porch Swing
"Armrests"
(2 qty.)
E

See Pattern Page 3 in Pattern Packet for full-size patterns.

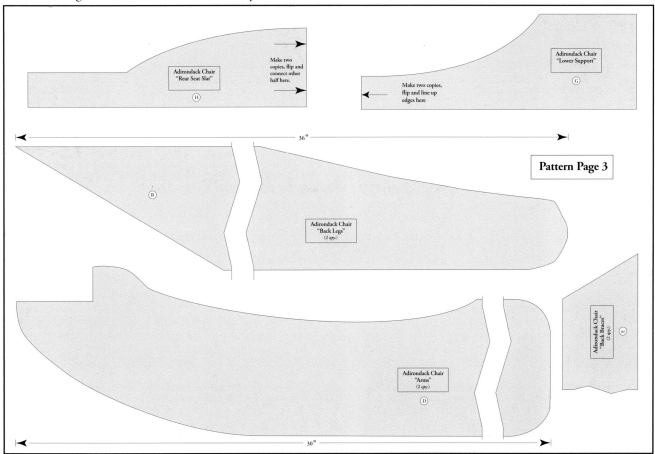

See Pattern Page 4 in Pattern Packet for full-size patterns.

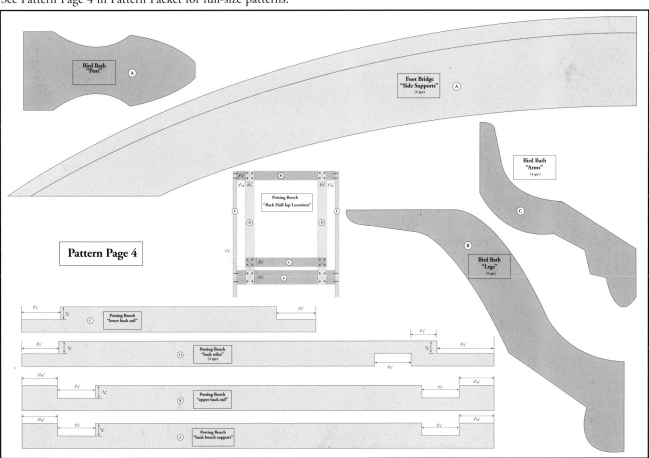

More Great Project Books from Fox Chapel Publishing

Woodworker's Pocket Reference
Everything a Woodworker Needs to Know at a Glance
by Charlie Self
Pages: 168
ISBN: 1-56523-239-9
$14.95

Fireplace and Mantel Ideas, 2nd edition
Build, Design and Install Your Dream Fireplace Mantel
by John Lewman
Pages: 196
ISBN: 1-56523-229-1
$19.95

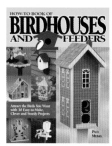

How-To Book of Birdhouses and Feeders
Attract the Birds You Want with 30 Easy to Make, Clever and Sturdy Projects
by Paul Meisel
Pages: 208
ISBN: 1-56523-237-2
$19.95

Woodworking Projects for Women
16 Easy-to-Build Projects for the Home and Garden
by Linda Hendry
Pages: 72
ISBN: 1-56523-247-X
$17.95

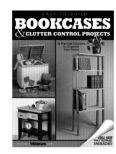

Easy-to-Build Bookcases and Clutter Control Projects
18 Practical Solutions to Organize Your Home
by The Editors of Weekend Woodcrafts Magazine
Pages: 144
ISBN: 1-56523-248-8
$17.95

Custom Wooden Boxes for the Scroll Saw
Innovative Techniques and Complete Plans 31 Projects
by Diana L. Thompson
Pages: 112
ISBN: 1-56523-212-7
$17.95

LOOK FOR THESE BOOKS AT YOUR LOCAL BOOK STORE OR WOODWORKING RETAILER

Or call 800-457-9112 • Visit www.FoxChapelPublishing.com

Learn from the Experts

Fox Chapel Publishing is not only your leading resource for woodworking books, we also publish the two leading how-to magazines for woodcarvers and woodcrafters!

WOOD CARVING ILLUSTRATED is the leading how-to magazine for woodcarvers of all skill levels and styles—providing inspiration and instruction from the some of the world's leading carvers and teachers. A wide range of step-by-step projects are presented in an easy-to-follow format, with great photography and useful tips and techniques. *Wood Carving Illustrated* delivers quality editorial on the most popular carving styles, such as realistic and stylized wildlife carving, power carving, Santas, caricatures, chip carving and fine art carving. The magazine also includes tool reviews, painting and finishing features, profiles on carvers, photo galleries and more.

SCROLL SAW WORKSHOP is the leading how-to magazine for novice and professional woodcrafters. Shop-tested projects are complete with patterns and detailed instructions. The casual scroller appreciates the in-depth information that ensures success and yields results that are both useful and attractive; the pro will be creatively inspired with fresh and innovative design ideas. Each issue of *Scroll Saw Workshop* contains useful news, hints and tips, and includes lively features and departments that bring the world of scrolling to the reader.

Want to learn more about a subscription? **Visit www.FoxChapelPublishing.com** and click on either the *Wood Carving Illustrated* button or *Scroll Saw Workshop* button at the top of the page. Watch for our special **FREE ISSUE** offer! Or call toll-free at 1-800-457-9112.